Keep this book as a constant compan..., ...uer, and resource that fuels your passion for teaching. You'll find yourself jotting down notes in the margins and within the thought-provoking prompts, then returning to it time and again for invaluable guidance.

—MaryAnn DeRosa, **Professor**
Curriculum Design Relay GSE;
International Education Consultant

Prendergast and Lee draw on a wealth of practical experience to provide insights and practical recommendations for educator resilience. By focusing on habits, they identify micro-changes that can have significant impact when applied consistently. This book should be an encouragement to educators.

—Jonathan Eckert, **Baylor University**
Center for School Leadership
Author of *Just Teaching: Feedback, Engagement,*
and Well-Being for Each Student

Habits of Resilient Educators is an invaluable tool that serves as a guide, playbook, and journal for educators. Dr. Lindsay Prendergast and Piper Lee set out to support teachers in reclaiming their why, while sharing research-based, best-practice habits of pedagogy. The interactive component makes this book deeply engaging and meaningful, and sure to provide the reader much clarity and insight.

—Abigail W. French, **CTE Pathway Coach**
Frederick County Public Schools, VA

It is refreshing to read *Habits of Resilient Educators* to remind yourself of the reasons you chose a career in education. This read provides strategies to get through the day-to-day challenges found in dealing with the demands of working within a school system. It helps to bring you back to the reason you are in the classroom in the first place by setting up procedures and adjusting your mindset about what an effective educator needs to do daily to continue to find joy in this career.

—Amanda S. Garman, **Principal**
R. B. Hunt Elementary School

Habits of Resilient Educators is a timely and well-needed book that examines the essential habits that educators must model, embrace, and identify in themselves to provide necessary social and emotional support and modeling for students. No matter if you are a new teacher or a veteran teacher, this resource provides myriad strategies to combat the challenges we often face day-to-day in schools.

—Brian Johnson, **Director of Learning Design and Development**

Teaching is complex, demanding, and challenging. Prendergast and Lee have not only crafted a collection of habits for teachers who have devoted their lives to giving back to their students and serving the education profession, but they have also extrapolated profound lessons based on their observations to help form healthy boundaries within the circles of this demanding profession.

—Debra Lane

Habits of Resilient Educators: Strategies for Thriving During Times of Anxiety, Doubt, and Constant Change by Dr. Lindsay Prendergast and Piper Lee is the ultimate lifeline for educators. This essential playbook, rich with practical, research-based strategies, equips seasoned and new educators to thrive amidst constant change. It's a must-have guide for reflective practitioners, mentors, and all educators navigating today's demanding educational landscape.

—Ann Marie Luce, **Associate Director Centennial Center for Leadership** Hobart and William Smith Colleges

Amidst overwhelming pressures in education, this book offers hope. Each chapter delves into a habit of resilience that can be explored in any sequence. Educators, from novice to veteran, will find strategies that empower them, helping them develop the inner strength and renewed energy necessary to positively impact their students.

—Carla Meyrink, **Co-founder and Director of The Community for Learning,** Santo Domingo, DR

The authors of *Habits of Resilient Educators* are trusted guides who—with authentic vignettes from the experiences of educators, reflection and planning opportunities, concrete examples, and important reframes that show us how to reconsider and check our assumptions—esteem the full personhood of educators. They hold knowledge and experience alongside empathy and hope during a time when this posture is particularly needed, and they invite readers on a growth journey that offers a vital blueprint for learning partnerships between educators and students.

—Afrika Afeni Mills, **Author**
Open Windows, Open Minds: Developing Antiracist,
Pro-Human Students

After reading this exhilarating text, I am better equipped as a leader to navigate a "Negative Nellie/Ned" and turn their negative energy into a contagious, positive mindset. Furthermore, as a building Principal, I am now more confident in working with my staff on building resilience, what it means to be resilient, and factors that contribute to an individual's resilience. This text is a MUST READ for all new and veteran teachers and school administrators!

—Melissa Roehm, **Principal**
Las Vegas, NV

I highly recommend this book for mentors and mentees. It will minimize anxiety for novice teachers and help them maintain their balance and thrive in the classroom. *Habits of Resilient Educators* encourages teachers to intentionally focus on what works, reflect on ways to stay inspired, and prioritize next steps.

—Carol Pelletier Radford, **Author,**
Teaching With Light: Ten Lessons for
Finding Wisdom, Balance and Inspiration, **and**
Founder, https://mentoringinaction.com/

Habits of Resilient Educators

Strategies for Thriving During Times of Anxiety, Doubt, and Constant Change

Lindsay Prendergast

Piper Lee

Foreword by Jeffrey D. Wilhelm

A Joint Publication

learningforward · nwea · CORWIN

FOR INFORMATION:

Corwin

A SAGE Company

2455 Teller Road

Thousand Oaks, California 91320

(800) 233-9936

www.corwin.com

SAGE Publications Ltd.

1 Oliver's Yard

55 City Road

London EC1Y 1SP

United Kingdom

SAGE Publications India Pvt. Ltd.

Unit No 323-333, Third Floor, F-Block

International Trade Tower Nehru Place

New Delhi 110 019

India

SAGE Publications Asia-Pacific Pte. Ltd.

18 Cross Street #10-10/11/12

China Square Central

Singapore 048423

Vice President and Editorial
  Director: Monica Eckman

Executive Editor: Tori Mello Bachman

Associate Content Development
  Editor: Sarah Ross

Editorial Assistant: Zachary Vann

Project Editor: Amy Schroller

Copy Editor: Karin Rathert

Typesetter: C&M Digitals (P) Ltd.

Cover Designer: Candice Harman

Marketing Manager: Margaret O'Connor

Printed in the United States of America

Library of Congress Cataloging-in-Publication Data

Names: Prendergast, Lindsay, author. | Lee, Piper, author.

Title: Habits of resilient educators : strategies for thriving during times of anxiety, doubt, and constant change / Lindsay Prendergast, Piper Lee; foreword by Jeffrey D. Wilhelm.

Description: Thousand Oaks, California : Corwin | NWEA, [2024] | Series: Corwin teaching essentials | Includes bibliographical references and index.

Identifiers: LCCN 2023046556 | ISBN 9781071919231 (paperback : acid-free paper) | ISBN 9781071932865 (epub) | ISBN 9781071932889 (epub) | ISBN 9781071932896 (pdf)

Subjects: LCSH: Motivation in education. | Reflective teaching. | Mindfulness (Psychology) | Resilience (Personality trait) | Habit. | Teachers—Psychology.

Classification: LCC LB1065 .P74 2024 | DDC 370.15/4—dc23/eng/20231201
LC record available at https://lccn.loc.gov/2023046556

This book is printed on acid-free paper.

SUSTAINABLE FORESTRY INITIATIVE | Certified Sourcing
www.sfiprogram.org
SFI-01028

24 25 26 27 28 10 9 8 7 6 5 4 3 2

Contents

Visit the *Habits of Resilient Educators* companion
website for downloadable resources.
resources.corwin.com/resilienteducators

Foreword

Teacher burnout is kind of like going broke: It happens gradually and then SUDDENLY. Here is the thing, though: If you burn out, it means that you were once on fire! Teaching is an intensely human endeavor. We deal with all of our students' needs AND the needs of parents, colleagues, and the community. Teaching is an endlessly enriching and enlivening pursuit that is also absolutely challenging, exhausting, and messy.

I tell my student teachers that joy and transformation are coming their way, so they need to learn to recognize these and celebrate them. But also coming their way are challenge and trouble. The questions are only how well they will prepare for the inevitable challenges, and how well will they respond.

I'm a passionate masters Nordic ski marathoner, and in our club's training room, there is a photo of the finish line of a World Cup Nordic ski race. The winner stands surrounded by seven other skiers who are all lying on the ground, visibly pained. Our coach has circled the standing victor and written in red marker: BE THIS SKIER! Through all the vagaries of teaching, that's what I want for all the teachers with whom I work: to be THAT teacher—the one who stands tall and strong amongst the slings and arrows. To achieve this, we need ritual structures and practices to help us pay mindful attention and develop equanimity and resilience. This book provides just such structures and rituals.

The book you hold in your hands is a great-hearted and generous book that provides the practices that will help you to achieve mindful, healthy, balanced wellness and thriving as a teacher over time. I'm currently entering my forty-first year of teaching (you can do the math). As I read this book, I recognized many of the habits that I have embraced throughout my career to thrive for this long—and learned many news one that I now embrace. Fifty years, here I come!

In the *Tassajara Bread Book*, Edward Brown writes of how as the baker at a Buddhist retreat, he was always dissatisfied with the biscuits he made. When he told his teacher that he never felt that his biscuits were quite right, his teacher asked, Compared to what? Brown realized that growing up he had only ever made

Pillsbury biscuits, the kind in the paper can that you crack open and the biscuits spill out perfectly formed onto your baking sheet. But to make biscuits from scratch is another matter involving many messy bowls and broken eggs and will result in some good old home-baked biscuits that can be fantastically tasty and flaky—or epic fails. The story illustrates many of the central points of this book: that impossible standards are harmful, that we all need to embrace the mess that brings us the real biscuit, that "perfection" is the enemy of the good, and that there is no perfect teacher so to be "good enough," as the psychologist D. W. Winnicott argues, is the healthiest goal and way to parent and teach.

This theme reminds me of Tom Newkirk's call to dismantle the myth of the superteacher; instead, give us stories of teachers who thrive in the turmoil, and show how they do it. (I love this book for this message alone.) But most of all, be your best possible and necessarily imperfect self in these wonderful and impossibly messy worlds of the classroom, school, and life. To achieve this, like any endurance athlete (and teachers are endurance athletes!), you must prepare, find supportive training and thinking partners, monitor your energy and fitness, know when to take breaks, and rehearse and refine your responses to challenges. In short, know how to "feed your legs" with routines that keep you nourished, rested, and strong.

When I finished reading this helpful book, I felt refreshed and forward looking, much like I feel after a long mindfulness meditation. Let me explain: In Buddhism, the central tenet is *metta*, often translated as loving kindness or friendliness. The first loving kindness must be to the self and with the recognition of the self's connection to all else. Self-care is essential to care for others. Loving kindness is contagious—if you care for yourself, respectfully and reflectively in the way this book suggests and supports you to do, it will spread to your students and colleagues. One of the Perfections in Buddhist teaching is "joyful effort." This generosity and joyful effort is evident in us as we teach well and in our students when they are engaged. Teaching strikes me as being very similar to parenting—impossibly joyful, with endless challenges and trouble, but worth it all and requiring joyful effort as we change diapers or deal with recalcitrant teens. As one Buddhist dharma has it, washing the dishes and carrying water is also your practice! The human heart, if you care for it, can have an endless capacity to love and to teach– which are much the same thing, I think. But it must be cared for.

As a teacher, you have many responsibilities. What I love about this book is that it teaches what you need to do to be responsible for your own heart, your own health, your own energy, attitude and response, and therefore for your own thriving—all of which is pre-requisite to doing the noble work of teaching. I know that like me, you will appreciate the thinking partnership and guidance this book provides to support us on our journeys as teachers.

—Jeffrey D. Wilhelm

Acknowledgments

First and foremost, this book is built upon the stories of countless wonderful, willing, and ever-inspiring teachers and leaders with whom we have worked. While there aren't enough pages to name them all, the lessons shared would not have been possible without their engagement with us as we attempted to support their work to reach all students. The leadership of our organization NWEA then provided us the moral and professional support to launch this project and accomplish this goal with the full backing of their tremendous resources. From brainstorming ideas, to peer edits, to constructive feedback, and also with a constant stream of encouragement, we share endless gratitude for fellow Corwin authors Dr. Chase Nordengren and Fenesha Hubbard, Robyn Sturgeon, Jacob Bruno, Dr. Erin Beard, Lindsay Deacon, and Kenny McKee.

And finally, we are both immeasurably grateful to our families for their endless and unwavering support. From the wordsmithing guidance of Lindsay's mother to Piper's patient children who held her accountable for deadlines and Lindsay's husband who constantly encouraged and supported, the pages before you are as much their sacrifices as ours.

PUBLISHER'S ACKNOWLEDGMENTS

Corwin gratefully acknowledges the contributions of the following reviewers:

Nicole Bell
Numeracy Consultant, Conseil Scolaire Acadien Provincial
Nova Scotia, Canada

Becky Evans
Educator, Lincoln Public Schools
Lincoln, NE

Oliver Woollett
Educator, St Leonard's College
Melbourne, Australia

About the Authors

Lindsay Prendergast has served schools and districts across the globe for nearly two decades as a leadership coach, consultant, principal, counselor, and teacher. She holds a master's degree in education administration from Colorado Western State University and a doctorate of education in education leadership from Wilkes University. Dr. Prendergast currently serves as Assistant Director of Learning Experiences for The Danielson Group (Framework for Teaching). While spending several post-pandemic years directly supporting nearly 30 principals as a leadership coach alongside Piper Lee, Lindsay spent hundreds of hours in classrooms observing teachers. These experiences, coupled with her expertise in instructional leadership and coaching, greatly informed the purpose of and need for this book. Lindsay enjoys advocating for educators by writing and speaking around the world for organizations such as ASCD, Learning Forward, Edutopia, AMLE, and others around instructional leadership grounded in student-centered schools where teachers thrive.

Piper Lee has more than twenty-five years of experience in education, including teaching, administration, instructional coaching, professional learning facilitation, and leadership coaching. Her passion for student and adult learning and improving effective teacher instruction and student success in learning ignited her pursuit of working as an instructional leadership coach nationally. Over the course of her career, Piper has served students, families, teachers, leadership teams, and undergraduate and graduate students. Most recently, Piper has been supporting district leaders, principals, and educators in one of the largest school districts in the country. While partnering with educators across the country, Piper has learned and lives the philosophy that rigorous relationships help to create transformative schools and impact every aspect of our lives. Piper received her bachelor of arts degree in Elementary Education, her master's degree in Curriculum and Instruction, and her education leadership certification and licensure from Winona State University in Minnesota.

Introduction

WHY THIS BOOK? WHY YOU?

In a contemporary teaching environment filled with stresses imposed by a generational pandemic, the already complex work of teaching has become even more challenging. Teachers today are faced with regular, unpredictable interruptions to learning, increasingly emotional demands from parents and caretakers, greater intervention by policymakers into curriculum and instruction, and an overall climate that cultivates fear, uncertainty, and doubt (FUD)—three psychological stressors known to spread false information and lead to apathy and burnout.

During a time when many educators are leaving the profession, others have rolled up their sleeves and are shining brightly through the challenges and pressures of the tumultuous education landscape. Countless others are just entering the field, eager to contribute and make an impact on the lives of their students. So we asked the question: What do teachers need to know and understand about the intersection of professional and personal practices to foster their own wellbeing while providing utmost effective teaching and learning in the classroom?

This book endeavors to present practices that meet the modern educator where they are: employed in a field at the intersection of mundanity and sainthood. The chapters ahead will guide you to examine research-proven teaching pedagogy and draw connections to how those practices, when implemented routinely within structures so that they become habits, can become optimal effective and efficient patterns in your professional life.

This book draws on our direct experience of more than forty combined years working in schools and districts. Most recently working as coaches alongside teachers and leaders around the globe, we observed firsthand how educators navigated making this new learning environment work for them. Throughout these pages, we draw on stories of resilience and clever adaptation to understand what being a high-functioning educator looks like in the twenty-first century and beyond. Combining these stories with a robust body of research on the habits of effective teaching and leadership, this book offers a rigorous and uplifting view of the difference educators can make even among all the contemporary stressors prevalent in schools.

Across the country, there is a sense of hopelessness around the ability to change this culture of chaos, and schools may struggle to find teachers for years to come. We must shift the narrative. Teaching can and should be a joyful profession where practitioners feel a sense of pride and accomplishment in their work. As a team of eternal optimists with deep experience and endless admiration for teachers, we aim to empower new and aspiring educators—or those with years of experience whose hope has waned—with a framework that enables them to regain control of their mindset and their practice despite the multitude of factors outside their control that they encounter daily.

THE INTERSECTION OF TEACHER AND STUDENT WELLBEING: WHAT THE RESEARCH SAYS

Education researcher John Hattie points to collective efficacy as one of the most impactful influences on student outcomes and the most consistently influential factor within teachers' control. Teacher collective efficacy is the belief held by teachers that they can make an impact on student performance (Goddard et al., 2020). This construct links to the broader observation of sociocultural theory, that we all have a broad network of influences that encourage or discourage us from believing in our ability to affect change. The habits of effective teaching described here all focus on creating a positive and supportive network of influences that can enable those beliefs for individual teachers and support them in creating that social context for their peers. In this way, we hope to show these habits aren't "life hacks" capable of solving any problem but small practices that collectively create a context within which teachers can grow and develop their own self-efficacy. This book will articulate strategies and practices that will support not only the preservation of teacher collective efficacy but ensure that it thrives.

Extending the importance of teacher self- and collective efficacy, research suggests that it also positively influences students' academic adjustment, overall job satisfaction for teachers, and even classroom quality. For example, studies have found that teacher self-efficacy may have a reciprocal effect on both teachers' and students' feelings of wellbeing and personal accomplishment (Bandura, 1997; Goddard et al., 2004). As you develop your own expertise and cultivate your wellbeing simultaneously, you are likely to extend the positive impacts of your efforts to the classroom environment and thus to your students. Teachers are more likely to experience high self-efficacy when they routinely practice self-regulation strategies—such as seeking help or support, setting goals, orienting their work toward mastery, or engaging in personal learning (Zee & Koomen, 2016). Bandura (1997) emphasized the crucial importance of teachers' beliefs that they have the skills and capabilities to selectively support their students where needed. The chapters within this book offer an opportunity to cultivate habits of behavior that build confidence by internalizing the thinking skills and high-frequency actions of teachers, such as making effective decisions or organizing immense amounts of complex information. In turn, teachers will be empowered to feel confident and capable of navigating any challenge they are faced with no matter the chaos of their surroundings or the uncertainty of what new challenges they'll face in the classroom tomorrow. The figure that follows shows the habits that resilient educators embody.

FIGURE 0.1

HOW YOUR HABITS INFLUENCE
YOUR IMPACT AS AN EDUCATOR

When you think of habits, perhaps you think of actions related to your personal life—managing your finances, exercising regularly, or perhaps even daily functions—such as always putting your car keys in the same place when you arrive home. Merriam-Webster (2023) defines a habit as, "a behavior pattern acquired by frequent repetition that shows itself in regularity or increased facility of performance." A habit must be acquired, indicating that to develop new habits we must be intentional about their development. Author Clear (2018) describes habits as "the compound interest of self-improvement" in his bestseller *Atomic Habits*, and it is upon this premise that we encourage you to approach your learning with this book. When you purposefully engage in the repetitive practice of behaviors or skills that have proven to have a positive impact on your wellbeing and on the learning outcomes of your students, they become seamless and so easy to implement that they cease to require much thought or precious energy. When these habits—a blend of personal behaviors applied to professional strategies—become automatic, they enable teachers to exert focus and effort on far more important and cognitively demanding priorities—such as the assessment of student learning. Embedding habits framed in these chapters—such as effective decision-making, avoiding negative influences, or cultivating mental resilience—provides the foundation upon which you can then easily overcome uncertainty and withstand constant ambiguity.

Further, habits are a catalyst for continuously improving your craft as a teacher and feeling confident and in control of your life. When the process of practicing new skills becomes less exciting or perhaps even boring, you'll know the novelty has dissipated; but this is a crucial time to persist. The intent is for these skills to become so easy and fluid that they are nearly mindless. When you cease to feel as though you are doing something unique or novel, it's time to celebrate a win—you've likely developed a new habit! Though perhaps seemingly minor, collectively developing the habits within these chapters will lead you toward mastery of an entire series of expert practices that will enable you to artfully navigate even the most cataclysmic changes to the school environment or field of education, as if you were effortlessly sailing along on a smooth sea.

HOW TO USE THIS BOOK

Whether you are reading this book independently or with the support of fellow educators around you, the chapters within are each an entry point into a multitude of opportunities to apply and practice the habit that you are examining. They are meant to be experienced in daily practice in order to fully immerse yourself in your personal understanding of what aspects of each habit yield the utmost outcomes for your growth as an educator.

In Chapter 1, you will examine how purpose connects to educator wellbeing and recognize where learning to develop the habit of returning to your *why* as an educator is critical to sustaining fulfillment and success in a career that possesses some of the highest rates of burnout.

Chapter 2 takes you on a journey through the unique merits of collaborating with others to understand not only why educators can elevate their impact by working together but how specific practices are proven to ensure collaboration moves beyond simply sharing work responsibilities.

In Chapter 3, we begin unpacking the habit of establishing and upholding high expectations for all students. By examining the influences of bias, for example, you will learn not only where to focus your efforts but how to do so in a consistent and intentional manner so that instruction is equitable for every student.

Chapter 4 explores the ever-important habit of utilizing data to drive decisions in the classroom. We will lift out straightforward, high-impact practices and streamline data processes to help you ensure your efforts to set high expectations for all students, for example, are utmost effective.

In Chapter 5, you will learn to apply the habit of utilizing routines and procedures across all areas of your teaching practice. In doing so, you set the stage to maximize effective use of your time and create opportunities for applying the remaining habits learned in the book.

Chapter 6 will begin bringing all of your newly developed habits from earlier chapters into the art of setting goals for your long-range personal and professional development. You'll recognize strategies for applying goal setting for both you and your students that ensure success for all.

In Chapter 7, you will spend time reflecting on your growth thus far through a focus on feedback. You will also learn how to seek and apply various sources of input and accelerate your growth journey.

If your learning around each habit thus far has you feeling daunted at the prospect of mastering them all, Chapter 8 will help you filter your learning and organize your efforts through the art of prioritization. You'll learn how to declutter both personal demands and professional ones.

As the book is situated to support you in navigating the new "normal" of education—constant fear, uncertainty, and doubt—Chapter 9 presents skills around the habit of avoiding negativity. You'll examine how to identify root causes of negative influences and apply skills in navigating them effectively so you may not only survive but thrive.

Chapter 10 concludes the book with the habit of developing and applying resilience. As a key factor to ensuring happiness, satisfaction, and fulfillment in your career as an educator, these final practices offer opportunities for application across each of the other habits in the book.

As you consider the content of the book, you'll recognize connections across each chapter that may compel you to return to the first chapter on "Clarify Your Why" for reflection opportunities even when you are deep into nearly the last chapter on "Prioritizing Amidst a Sea of Initiatives." Let the learning progression evolve organically for you—no need to proceed methodically from one chapter to the next unless that best suits your interest! For maximum effect, step away from reading the chapter pages to put the strategies into practice in your classroom or office. Then, return to reflect on the experience and delve into the next activity for even deeper learning about the chapter's habit of focus.

TAKE YOURSELF ON A PERSONAL GROWTH JOURNEY

If you find yourself reading this book on your own, consider it your new companion to lead you toward the exciting goal of thriving, not just surviving, as an educator. Test your confidence, expand your imagination, and challenge conventional wisdom around how teachers are expected to mindlessly function under exorbitant levels of stress for the duration of their career. You'll engage in research-proven practices that help you organize your time, streamline your efficiency, and maximize your impact on student learning outcomes. Leverage the activities in the "Setting Goals" chapter, for example, as you practice new skills in utilizing data to drive your decision-making processes from Chapters 3 and 8, and become a master of propelling your own learning as well as your students' learning.

COLLABORATE WITH A
MENTOR, COACH, PLC, OR COHORT

The content of this book lends itself well to application in a setting with the perspective and expertise of fellow educators around you. Whether you are working through the chapters in an induction program, reading the book with a professional learning community (PLC) in your school or district, or teaming up with a mentor to support your learning, it's important to situate your approach with a mindset of collaboration and a focus on growth. Despite the tremendous expertise you certainly bring with you to the learning journey, be ready to set aside assumptions and preconceived ideas about your ability to become even better. To create new habits or routines in your practice, you'll likely need to disrupt existing patterns and beliefs, and that can be challenging or even uncomfortable. We recommend setting learning intentions each time you engage in reading a new chapter or collaborating with others around what you are learning. Prioritize being open, receptive, and curious, and you will maximize the impact of your learning journey for yourself and for your students!

REFLECTION

Get Ready, Set Your Intentions, and Go Improve!

MY LEARNING INTENTIONS FOR READING THIS BOOK ARE...
1.
2.
3.

CHAPTER 1

Clarify Your Why
Purpose as a Habit

Abby, a middle school social studies teacher, has been managing her teaching career, single motherhood, a new school, and multiple community traumas ever since the COVID-19 global pandemic shifted everything in March of 2020. The challenges have often felt insurmountable, so much so she felt her passion for teaching waning at times, and she had never imagined this to be a possibility. As the school year progressed, revisiting her purpose as an educator helped mitigate frustrations. Feeling particularly overwhelmed on a Sunday evening and thinking of ALL the expectations for the new week, Abby developed a simple meditation: Remembering how easily my emotions and attitude can impact or transfer to my students, I choose a mindset centered in compassion and empathy. I will meet people where they are, honoring who they are and what they need. That is my purpose.

WHY PURPOSE MATTERS

In a workplace environment, professionals are considered fortunate if they spend their career engaged in work that aligns with their personal values. In education, however, there exists an underlying assumption that teachers are inherently devoted to a higher calling—to a purpose that serves a noble, greater good. True, education is a field that is rich with the opportunity to make an impact on the lives of individuals or even society, and thus teachers experience the rewards of serving others. In fact, teaching is regularly listed in the top tiers of most rewarding jobs in the world (Intuit, 2022). Yet teachers may find themselves conflicted upon encountering unforeseen challenges or impediments to their ability to achieve the goal of making a difference for every child. This can be disheartening or perplexing. Thus, it's important to understand the distinction between a purpose placed on your shoulders by outside entities and one you derive for yourself and that is aligned to who *you* are.

This chapter explores purpose as a journey, not a fixed focal point. Purpose, as it relates to the profession of teaching, does not always lead to feeling excited about the daily work at hand in the classroom, nor is it a cure for burnout. There are benefits to examining and embracing purpose that will contribute to such outcomes, yes. In fact, research highlights the powerful value of identifying your purpose as having a positive impact on your wellbeing, your motivation, and even your sense of agency (Schaefer et al., 2013; Vos & Vitali, 2018). However, finding fulfillment as an educator connects more directly to recognizing your capacity to have a direct and positive impact on others and then aligning your daily actions and decisions to your unique, personal purpose. By prioritizing the explicit purpose you aspire to achieve—embedding social-emotional learning into all academic curriculum, for example, or elevating society's respect for teachers on a broad level—you serve yourself as well as the greater good. This becomes a habit, a form of routine, through which we consistently approach our work. Whether planning instruction, evaluating student learning, or collaborating with colleagues, we move toward this goal by grounding our efforts in the response to this singular question: Why?

PURPOSE IS . . .	PURPOSE IS NOT . . .
• Grounded in your personal beliefs, values, and needs	• Determined by others around you
• A source of motivation when challenges arise or obstacles occur	• Always easy to identify or strongly evident
• Something that may evolve over time based on new experiences	• An objective to be accomplished

Finding fulfillment as an educator connects more directly to recognizing your capacity to have a direct and positive impact on others and then aligning your daily actions and decisions to your unique, personal purpose.

A theme you will hear resonate throughout this book is this: Teaching is complex, demanding, and challenging. It is not for the faint of heart. Further, the distance between what teaching is perceived to encompass by those outside the profession (yes, also those aspiring to become teachers) and the reality of a teacher's daily experience is vast. Those arriving in the profession without an existing conviction that it is exactly what they always dreamt of doing may find themselves apprehensive about the future. Perhaps you once felt a strong grasp of your goal to contribute to the betterment of others through becoming a teacher and are overwhelmed by the volatile environment surrounding education today. Or you may be reading this, blissfully existing in teacher-Nirvana and wondering, "What's the big deal about *why*?" No matter the reason, there will be something here for you.

Purpose connects deeply to our ability to embrace our value as an educator; to persist in the face of challenging circumstances, of which there are many; and to give our utmost best to the students in our care. Answering the question *why*? is more acutely personal than it may appear. Educators are susceptible to external perspectives around why you teach. Society tells the world that you are noble servants, yet sometimes the job is frustrating, boring, anxiety-inducing, or even sad. So what do you do when society doesn't accept that you don't love your job as a teacher or when you are asked to project something different than you feel or believe? The answer is to lean into purpose. *Your* purpose.

UNPACKING YOUR PURPOSE

At some point in the process of finding a job as a teacher, you were probably asked, "What excites you about teaching?" to dig into your intrinsic motivation for teaching. There is a high likelihood that teaching will be rewarding both for you, the teacher, and for the hundreds of students you will encounter over the years. However, there will come a time—or many times—when faced with the complexities and demands of the daily work, not to mention the myriad societal problems that teachers encounter within a classroom and are ill-equipped to resolve, that you'll have a different question: Is it worth it? When teachers find their original purpose at odds with their ability to withstand the systemic challenges of the work, they may feel powerless, defeated, or hopeless.

For the first eight years of her teaching career, Erin primarily taught secondary English language arts classes—Grades 7, 8, and 9. She felt the tensions between her love of learning and the arts (including language arts) clash with the pressure of No Child Left Behind (NCLB) legislation plus other accountability expectations.

(Continued)

(Continued)

Too often, external pressures felt like they ate up what she found to be her higher purpose: supporting students to grow a lifelong love of learning and creating. To navigate out of that paralyzing tension, she learned how she and her students could still meet the expectations while also attaining a higher purpose. For example, she learned how to closely read the content standards and the standardized test blueprints to look for project-based ways to attain those expectations while also cultivating joy, curiosity, and whole-human growth (not just academic achievement). Erin and her students were much happier and successful when she learned how to look at the expectations in this way.

The antidotes to futility, defeat, or hopelessness are power (the kind where you control your own destiny, not the lives of others!), accomplishment, and inspiration. To zero in on something that gives you purpose, begin by identifying ways that you can spend your time that you believe are important. Begin by asking yourself the following question: What makes me feel that my talents are benefiting the world? Use the boxes that follow to brainstorm the ways you have (or ways you can in the future) dedicated your efforts that may provide value to you or to others.

EXAMPLE: MENTORING NEW TEACHERS	EXAMPLE: IMPROVING THE CAMPUS GARDEN			

Now, examine the underlying purpose behind some of those activities. Take note: Some of those activities are perfunctory in purpose and that's OK. Not every single work-related task carries the connection to purpose; some things are mandated or simply operational in nature. Let's look a bit closer, though, at those that strike you as personally meaningful or related to an area where you know you are using your particular talents. For example, consider that an activity you listed in the matrix was "designing the common assessments used by your department/ grade level." Now use these questions to unpack the underlying impact such an action could have.

REFLECTION

WHY do you believe this is important?

_____

_____

_____

WHO is impacted, or benefits, by this?

_____

_____

_____

HOW are each of those individuals or groups impacted?

_____

_____

_____

WHAT happens if this is not done?

_____

_____

_____

(Continued)

(Continued)

WHAT skill(s) do you possess that enables you to accomplish this?

_____

_____

_____

WHAT are the emotions you experience by engaging in this action?

_____

_____

_____

WHAT makes you uniquely suited to accomplish this?

_____

_____

_____

By examining the greater implications of even a seemingly mundane action, you will begin to see the reason you pursue it. It's easy to dismiss our actions as always being "just part of the job" or "my boss told me it was required" when, in fact, there are likely countless things you do without being asked. In this example, the impact you believe your expertise could influence is *ensuring every student receives a rigorous, fair, and equitable chance to achieve high-learning outcomes.* This is an impact that supersedes a benevolent effort to do work that is required so that other colleagues can have more free time. This is an impact that may reflect or reveal a purpose to which you can more intentionally align with other areas of your practice. As a result, your work becomes more meaningful and connected to your own personal journey toward finding value in the daily work at hand.

CONNECT TO YOUR IMPACT ON A BROADER SCALE

When you are able to directly see or feel the effect of your efforts in the classroom, your motivation naturally increases. That said, there are countless days when you may not experience the reward of knowing you had an impact. Zeroing in on what you want your impact to be can mitigate the risk of burnout and increase hopefulness.

CONNECTION

In Chapter 6, you'll learn about goal setting practices, which also support your purpose.

Earlier, you practiced determining your purpose as a teacher. Purpose, however, without a plan for enabling it to guide your journey is likely to land you right where you started: apprehensive and uncertain about the future. By applying backward planning strategies, you can identify an explicit outcome of fulfilling your purpose: impact.

How is your purpose connected to the impact you aspire to make as an educator? Refer to the notes you took in the previous brainstorm boxes and the reflection questions that follow to map your personal impact aspirations.

REFLECTION

Who has had an impact on me?

_____

_____

_____

On whom do I wish to have an impact?

_____

_____

_____

What actions can I take in the next five years to ensure I achieve this impact?

_____

_____

_____

Connect your impact plan to your classroom. Imagine you could only teach ONE lesson to your students! Complete the following prompts:

REFLECTION

What impact would you want that lesson to have on the lives of your students?

_____

_____

_____

What would that lesson be (it may or may not be related to the content or subject you typically teach)?

_____

_____

_____

How would you know if your lesson had the impact you intended?

_____

_____

_____

What step(s) can you take beginning right now to infuse your teaching practice with the impact you aspire to have on your students?

_____

_____

_____

HOW PURPOSE EVOLVES AND WHY IT MATTERS

Teachers enter the profession for a multitude of reasons and at diverse points in their working life. You may have followed a spouse to a new community and found the school district was hiring through an alternative-licensure program, or perhaps you knew you would be a teacher from a very young age. No matter the origin, your purpose for becoming a teacher—for a job, as a career path, or to follow a higher calling—also offers unique insights into how you approach the work and ways that you may leverage your beliefs to feel the most satisfied and rewarded over time.

Consider the uniquely meaningful—and valid—purpose that an educator may identify depending on how they view the day-to-day work.

	PURPOSE	STRENGTHS	CHALLENGES
Teaching as a job	Engaged in the work for the purpose of necessity in order to support their personal needs or a household Finds high value in work benefits, such as schedule or calendar	Better able to set boundaries around their work and professional life Less susceptible to emotional turbulence from job-related stress	Risk of being perceived as less committed to the school or students
Teaching as a career	Engaged in the work for the purpose of growth and development of skills and relationships	Sees growth opportunities within challenges Engages in all aspects of the school community as a participant or leader	May become disillusioned with the work if not receiving personal rewards, such as promotions or accomplishments
Teaching as a calling	Engaged in the work to participate in serving a societal improvement effort (alleviating generational poverty, eliminating illiteracy, etc.)	Feels high levels of excitement and passion for the job despite challenges and demands	At risk for over-sacrificing personal wellbeing to complete work May inadvertently impose beliefs and expectations on students or colleagues (martyr behavior)

It's incredibly important to understand that the purpose you originally developed upon entering the field of teaching may evolve over time. More accurately understanding your beliefs about the purpose of your work at different junctures of your career bolsters your ability to withstand the threats you will encounter to always finding teaching to be a fulfilling, rewarding profession.

Understanding your beliefs about the purpose of your work at different junctures of your career bolsters your ability to withstand the threats you will encounter to always finding teaching to be a fulfilling, rewarding profession.

Teaching is a profession that is often attractive to those who value helping or serving others, so it is important for teachers to recognize the ways in which a benevolent personality-type can be more susceptible to discouragement, stress, or even being taken advantage of. Just as research suggests that teaching is one of the most rewarding professions in the world (Intuit, 2022), other studies—even many prior the COVID-19 pandemic—highlight that teaching is one of the most stressful occupations, with comparisons to emergency room doctors, among others (Greenberg et al., 2017). If a teacher doesn't believe they should sacrifice their personal wellbeing for the benefit of their students, they may be susceptible to feelings of guilt resulting from societal pressures and perceptions around teaching as a "calling." Guilt can dissolve personal boundaries and lead teachers to overwork to meet the unrelenting demands of the job—and ultimately to burnout, dissatisfaction, or hopelessness.

CONNECTION

You'll learn strategies for resisting the pull of negative attitudes and perceptions in Chapter 9.

Because society perpetuates the perception of teachers as selfless souls, there are ample external pressures that may influence your belief that any one of these purposes—job, career, or calling—is superior to the other. As Dampf (2022) shares in *It's About Skillsets and Support, Not Sainthood*, "'passionate' teaching is not the same as skillful teaching, and our love of the saint obscures our view of the skill." As a professional educator, acknowledging your belief about why you do the work each and every day creates the opportunity to maximize your strengths and mitigate your limitations to preserve your utmost precious commodity: your efficacy.

Use the questions that follow to reflect on your purpose.

REFLECTION

Which of the purposes (job, career, or calling) did you most closely align with when you began your work as a teacher? Is it the same today as you read this book?

_____

_____

_____

What factors may have influenced the presence or absence of any changes?

_____

_____

_____

ALIGNING YOUR PURPOSE TO EQUITABLE PRACTICES

Identifying and embracing your purpose as a teacher presents a rich opportunity to recognize that you are capable and competent and that you provide a critically valuable service to other people. However, there is a delicate balance between serving others with our talents and failing to recognize that our students and colleagues bring ample skills and understandings of their own to the relationship. When we engage in helping others, it's important to understand we are not morally or socially superior to those we serve, nor are we in this position to "fix" our students or colleagues, as this can have harmful effects on those we are helping. For example, research suggests a savior complex can inadvertently prevent the recipient of support or assistance from developing their independence and command of skills (Aronson, 2017). Further, to fully embrace the potential of our students and teammates, we must seek to understand the profoundly valuable assets they possess.

To fully embrace the potential of our students and teammates, we must seek to understand the profoundly valuable assets they possess.

Examining deficit ideology provides a meaningful next step to understanding the way our language and beliefs merit close examination in tandem with determining our purpose. Deficit ideology is "a way of blaming the victim, of justifying outcome inequalities by pointing to 'deficiencies' in marginalized communities. It justifies oppression by placing those being oppressed as the problem—and by pointing to the oppressors as the solution" (Baker, 2020).

Further reading on this topic is a tremendous opportunity to more deeply understand ways to align your purpose to equitable practices and could begin with Gorski and Swalwell's (2023), _Fix Injustice, Not Kids and Other Principles for Transformative Equity Leadership._

To foster clarity around the why behind our why, Hubbard (2023), author of _The Equity Expression: 6 Entry Points for Nonnegotiable Academic Success,_ describes the importance of manifesting equitable actions and attitudes in everything we do as a teacher, including pursuit of our purpose. The entry points to equity in Hubbard's book describe opportunities where equitable practices might be considered or enhanced, including the following:

- mindsets
- relationships
- processes
- products
- spaces
- systems

When thinking about the importance of purpose as related to equity, the entry points of mindsets, relationships, and processes are especially applicable.

> **Mindsets:** Think about the "mental attitudes that determine how [you] interpret and respond to situations" (Hammond, 2014, p. 157). Consider your own beliefs about teaching and learning, content, pedagogy, and students. What assumptions, attitudes, or biases do you recognize?

FIGURE 1.1

Source: Hubbard, F. (2023). *The equity expression: 6 entry points for nonnegotiable academic success.* Corwin.

An inequitable mindset: During a data analysis conversation, a seventh-grade teacher predicts that boys would not score well, noting that girls have better reading skills and work habits, which would influence their test scores.

An equitable mindset: A first-grade teacher reviews her curriculum resources as she begins planning for instruction. She notices that every story in the unit is centered around characters of one gender and one race, eliminating the opportunity for many students in her class to feel represented in their learning experiences. She seeks additional resources tied to the grade-level standard that include diverse characters throughout.

Relationships: Examine your relationships with students, teachers, and school leaders. How do you ensure that those relationships are psychologically safe and learner oriented and that they promote collaborative inquiry?

An inequitable relationship: A student is sleeping in class, and the teacher scolds them publicly for not being attentive then issues a written reprimand for misconduct.

An equity-focused relationship: A student is sleeping in class. The teacher discreetly asks the student if they're OK, reminding them of the classroom norms for engagement. Later in the day, the teacher meets individually with the student to ask about the obstacles impeding their attentiveness during class.

Processes: Assess the routines, procedures, and protocols you use in your day-to-day teaching and learning. How do you incorporate systemic processes into your classroom environment? The changes can be minor—like how you ask students to get in line—or major—like how you choose which topics to teach and when.

Inequitable process: To address the unfinished learning that students need support with, a teacher's lessons focus on the prerequisite skills from the previous grade, not on grade-level skills.

An equitable process: The students do grade-level work, and the teacher prioritizes the prerequisite skills to be addressed as scaffolding planned within grade-level lessons.

EMPLOYING YOUR WHY
IN THE CLASSROOM

When connecting your purpose as an educator to your daily work, intentionally integrating specific practices will ensure success. For example, by routinely conducting an inventory of the ways you provide feedback to students through the lens of your purpose to ensure every student experiences equitable instruction, you are able to identify successful practices as well as where to make periodic adjustments.

There are three key strategies you can implement right now and, as a regular practice moving forward, use to elevate the integration of purpose in the classroom. They are the following:

- Plan for purpose
- Communicate purpose
- Share your purpose

PLAN FOR PURPOSE

Infusing teaching and learning with purpose begins with intentional planning for integration. While your lesson plans likely include space for learning outcomes, assessments, and activities, do you take the time to evaluate *why* you chose to utilize each of the specific tools and resources that will bring those plans to life? Practice pulling out a lesson plan (sourced from the school curriculum or created by you or a willing colleague) in a collaborative planning meeting and move through each section of the plan, one at a time, answering the question *why* as you read it.

Analyze a lesson plan and select the learning tasks you would use with your students. Use this chart to guide your analysis.

QUESTION	RESPONSE	CHANGES TO CONSIDER
Why was this learning task identified as the best choice to use with students?		

QUESTION	RESPONSE	CHANGES TO CONSIDER
Why do students need to learn this, and how will this (assessment, activity, etc.) deliver on that goal?		
Why is this the most appropriate standard to teach at this time?		

COMMUNICATE PURPOSE

Studies have shown that relevance increases learner engagement, particularly in older students, since as far back as the early twentieth century when Dewey (1913) wrote *Interest and Effort in Education*. John Hattie's research also highlights the incredible impact that occurs when learners understand the intention of what they are learning. It has an effect size of 0.88 (0.4 being the mean) (Clarke, 2021). It's easy, however, to rest on the assumption that because we know why something is important, those around us do as well. When it comes to your students, that may rarely be the case!

Begin by getting an understanding of whether you practice the habit of communicating purpose to your students. Do you tell them why they are learning a particular concept, why they are being asked to engage in an activity, or why the learning is progressing in a certain order? Over the course of a school day, keep a notepad nearby and write a tick mark, a check, or some other symbol each time you notice that you share the purpose of any activity with your students (even tasks like lining up in order or waiting for others to finish before beginning to speak, for example!). Use the tracking chart to set incremental goals for increasing the practice and to gather data at periodic intervals—once a week, for example—until the practice becomes internalized!

Practice: _____

TOTAL TIMES PURPOSE COMMUNICATED	GOAL	BY WHAT DATE?

Day 1	Day ____	Day ____	Day____	Day ____	Day ____	Day ____

SHARE YOUR PURPOSE

Have you ever stopped to consider what students believe about you as a teacher and why you design instruction or create a classroom environment the way you have? Sharing your personal purpose with students—not the purpose of the Socratic Seminar they're engaging in but rather why you serve as an educator—is likely to incite their recognition that you care for them and potentially open pathways to stronger relationships. This doesn't have to be a formal event in which you garner the full attention (unless that's your style) of the class but can be as simple as infusing intentional conversations into your interactions with students.

Start small: With the whole class (at any age group), share one of the reasons you became an educator and connect that reason to why you chose a specific activity the students will engage in as it relates to your purpose.

Engage with individuals: Tell students you will be asking them to each share (in whatever format makes most sense) the ways they believe you can most effectively help them succeed. Incorporate these suggestions as appropriate into instruction, assessments, resources, and so forth, and articulate that you made that intentional choice because you knew it was important to a student.

Gather data: Before coming to any conclusions on your own about what you think students perceive as your why as a teacher, ask them! This may be more effective with older students who could likely develop a thoughtful answer—but not always. Conduct an anonymous survey or poll to gather their ideas. Beware of the inclination to respond publicly to the private answers to avoid the risk of embarrassing anyone, but use the data to craft your next explicit actions to communicate your authentic purpose to your students and enjoy their appreciation for taking their ideas to heart!

For further reading on the research-proven practices around sharing learning intentions and success criteria with students or around teacher credibility as these areas relate to your purpose, check out the following:

The Teacher Clarity Playbook, Doug Fisher and Nancy Frey, 2018, Corwin.

The Teacher Credibility and Collective Efficacy Playbook, Grades K–12, Douglas Fisher, Nancy Frey, and Dominique Smith, 2020, Corwin.

GETTING YOUR GROOVE BACK: WHAT TO DO WHEN YOUR WHY BECOMES FUZZY

Reading this chapter may elicit emotions of inspiration, curiosity, or excitement. Or perhaps it left you feeling uncertain and wondering: what if I really cannot find my purpose as a teacher? Or what if I cannot muster the enthusiasm for my work anymore, no matter how clear my purpose seems? The following approaches can help you navigate these emotions and experiences.

COME BACK LATER

The list of "should" is long in your life, and while you appreciate the value in finding your purpose as a teacher, perhaps it seems like one more item on an already lengthy task list. Although these activities are aimed at bringing clarity and calm to your hectic life, choose to give yourself permission to come back to them later if they currently increase your tension levels! Or set a very low-key action plan to try one activity per week or per month, and gauge how your emotional reserves are handling the load. If returning to this chapter later strikes you as a more comfortable step, consider alternatives that may elevate your wellbeing first.

RECONNECT WITH OLD PASSIONS

If nothing in your current work is inspiring you, reflect on a time when you truly loved your work as a teacher. While you may not be able to replicate a former school or group of students, examine the conditions surrounding that experience:

- Who was involved?
- What were your favorite things to be working on?
- Who was around you at the time?
- What rewards did you gain from the type of work you were doing (personal satisfaction, student achievement, accolades from others, etc.)?

Amongst your answers, look for connections to people, things, and actions that you could use to reinvigorate in your present environment. Did you love working on the school data committee and your current school does not have one? Seek your supervisor to discuss initiating a new group. Were you co-teaching with an inspiring colleague and there isn't enough staff for this anymore? Initiate a mentoring relationship with a newer teacher to co-plan with and observe each other's lessons, or seek a colleague on staff to be your mentor for the same!

SEEK THE SUPPORT OF OTHERS

In Chapter 2, you will learn about the incredible value of collaboration to withstand the risk of becoming very isolated as a teacher. This practice does not solely pertain to planning instruction but to the camaraderie and companionship that bolsters your ability to endure challenging times in your career. Chances are you are not the only one who is drifting or feeling a bit lackluster. Consider starting a book club with interested colleagues about a non-education related topic. Or ask your supervisor if they are aware of anyone who may be feeling disheartened by the work at hand, and reach out for a coffee to see if your experiences may provide one another some opportunities for mutual support.

TRY MINDFULNESS PRACTICES

Mindfulness does not mean solely meditation or practicing yoga—though these are very effective forms of mindfulness practice! Mindfulness is a range of strategies and actions that foster inner calm, a sense of awareness of self, and feelings of control over our environment. Reflective journaling, for example, and breathing exercises are ways to cultivate mindfulness and promote mental clarity and calm. If you're feeling distracted, stressed, overwhelmed, exhausted, or all of the above, examine basic mindfulness practices to help regain happiness and peace. Using a website, such as mindful.org can also provide further ideas.

The Big Ideas

As you delve deeper into this book, consider what you learned about the importance of clarifying your purpose here. Thus far you have explored the value of examining and identifying your personal purpose as a teacher, recognizing that this may evolve over time and there is no one perfect or final answer. You learned steps for engaging your purpose in the classroom through planning and also in connecting with students and how to align your actions with equity.

Use the activities within Chapter 1 at different times or stages in your career. Create a notebook where you may keep a record of each addition to even further enhance reflection opportunities around your personal growth and development. You'll notice as you read further that each of the chapters presents a unique opportunity to connect your practices to your purpose, too.

Let's Reflect

What surprised you about the ideas you generated about your purpose within this chapter?

_____

_____

_____

What were the differences and/or similarities between your current beliefs about purpose and those you held when you first began teaching?

_____

_____

_____

What are you still wondering about as it relates to applying purpose to your work as a teacher?

_____

_____

_____

What's Next?

In Chapter 2, you will dig deep into the skills used in collaboration and examine the importance of connecting with colleagues of various roles and experience levels to not only fend off isolation but to grow as a professional. Future chapters will guide you on a learning journey through setting goals, seeking and applying feedback for your personal and professional growth, and applying procedures and routines to all areas of your work. Equipped with new understandings around your purpose as an educator, get ready to now maximize your impact alongside others through collaboration.

CHAPTER 2

Collaborate
Don't Isolate!

Selah had returned to her second-grade classroom after teaching virtually for a year and half during the COVID-19 pandemic. It had been over eighteen months since Selah could sit in the same room and collaborate with her colleagues. She had never really liked or disliked grade-level meetings or professional learning communities prior to the pandemic. However, Selah found herself very emotional during the first "in-person" meeting. As Selah described the experience, she began to beam as she recapped the gift of being able to collaborate with "the brilliant minds and caring hearts," as she termed her colleagues.

Selah and her colleagues shared how they had a new appreciation for the opportunity to work side by side with other educators. They also reflected on the many benefits that came from virtual meetings. However, Selah and her colleagues shared that prior to the pandemic, they had often worked in silos and that virtual meetings during the pandemic period had really reinforced this isolated or silo style of teaching and navigating challenges. The team also shared that through the isolation and heavy lifting they were each having to do alone, the planning for lessons and analyzing data had become incredibly challenging. The team had a new understanding of how powerful working collaboratively together was.

Once back together in the school building, during their initial meetings, Selah's team took time to set up new norms and a mission statement. They wanted to make sure that everyone felt valued, seen, and heard, and they wanted to ensure that collaboration would be at the heart of their work and experience as educators. Selah's grade-level team wanted to move from planning lessons in isolation to collaborating, analyzing data, problem-solving, sharing their ideas, and distributing the overall workload. They also had rich conversations about recognizing Helen Keller's (1933) famous words, "Alone we can do little, together we can do much."

WHY COLLABORATION
IS IMPORTANT

Collaboration means working together. Typically, collaboration is the process of two or more individuals working together to achieve a common task or objective. Effective and efficient collaboration requires clear and kind communication, interpersonal skills, knowledge sharing, and teamwork. There are also many benefits for educators when collaborating and operating as a team with a clear vision on a learning objective or task, such as positive impact on team relationships, increased work efficiency and productivity, and employee satisfaction. Ultimately, when teachers are collaborating, they will have a positive impact on one another, and this will contribute to positive school culture and student achievement improvements.

Andrew Carnegie, a captain of industry in nineteenth-century America, described teamwork as the ability to come together toward a common vision and to direct individual accomplishments toward organizational objectives.

Examples of teachers collaborating might include working in grade-level teams, sharing work responsibilities, and providing feedback to one another for lesson planning or instructional rounds. Regular interactions with colleagues or mentors are crucial to building trust and forming and maintaining lasting relationships; collaboration requires commitment by every member of the team to prioritize these interactions. Teachers can feel isolated when spending most of the time alone in classrooms with students, but developing a consistent schedule to meet as a grade-level team or in professional learning communities and committing to that meeting time allows teachers to feel valued and heard regularly. When teachers can connect frequently and are accountable to one another for this regular meeting time, a trusting and more confident collaborative team forms.

COLLABORATION IN EDUCATION IS . . .	COLLABORATION IN EDUCATION IS NOT . . .
• All participants sharing creatively toward achieving a goal	• One teacher sharing what has always been done in the past around a specific task
• All teachers unpacking a standard and using new and old resources to align to the student learning task	• Veteran teachers talking about a standard and then sharing materials to be used with new teachers
• Several people sharing ideas and solving problems collectively	• One voice dominating the conversation
• Analyzing grade-level formative and summative assessments to make instructional decisions for "our" students	• One teacher analyzing data in isolation to make instructional decisions for "their" students

SHARING OUR SUPERPOWERS
WITH ONE ANOTHER

Effective grade-level or content teams can be likened to the Marvel Superhero team. Each Marvel character possesses a unique gift that is intended to protect planet Earth. However, they are also seen collaborating and working together to fight the good fight. When the Marvel team comes together and combines their powers, they can more effectively and efficiently overcome evil in the world. The type of challenge the Marvel team faces determines which superheroes fight on the front lines and which ones are there for support. Within each specific battle, even the characters on the front line can change depending on the strengths or superpowers needed. The supporting role is essential, as we often see superheroes using their unique strengths to help one another as they battle the impossible forces. Therefore, each Marvel hero has a significant role on the team, and the vision of keeping Earth safe is always at the center of all decisions. The Marvel team may not always agree, but they have their code of conduct that helps them to fix their eyes on the goal of protecting Earth.

Relatively, all educators possess strengths, and when they come together and collaborate with a common vision, they can accomplish what may seem impossible. An example of this might be veteran teachers sharing pedagogical moves in a content area while newer teachers share creative ways of integrating technology and media in Tier 1 instruction. Another example might be a team planning for instruction while unpacking grade-level standards. When the team collectively leans in and learns from one another, they can productively identify what the standard is asking students to master. It is common for teachers to know instructional groups of standards generally but not all of them masterfully. The powerful move of collectively and collaboratively unpacking and investigating standards allows all teachers to gain pedagogical tools and a deeper understanding of the appropriate level of rigor when instructing students. This practice of collectively analyzing standards allows teachers to fix their eyes on the goal of supporting growth and achievement for all students.

Comparatively, it is important for all stakeholders on a team to have a voice and share their superpowers when thinking about the "strategic plan" of providing access to Tier 1 instruction for all students. New members to a team often bring a different way of thinking about doing things. It is important that these new ideas are heard and valued by the veteran team members when planning for instruction. When teachers honor that their peers may possess unique qualities they can all learn from, the team will be able to accelerate growth and achievement for all students. This work may seem impossible at times, but just like the Marvel superheroes, when teachers share their superpowers and encourage one another, they can conquer the mission of helping all students to accelerate their learning.

> *When teachers honor that their peers may possess unique qualities they can all learn from, the team will be able to accelerate growth and achievement for all students.*

Here are some ways teams can learn more about each other's strengths so that they can work effectively and efficiently:

- Observe one another teaching and share a "superpower" you noticed and want to use in your own classroom.
- Spend time taking some personality assessments like Strength Finder 2.0. or Enneagram personality tests and share out results with your team. Discuss how the personality assessments could help you work more effectively.
- Discuss who the creative geniuses, organizers, activators, data analysts, and connectors are on the team.
- Share professional and personal goals that you are setting for the year. Think about how you can support one another's learning and work.
- Discuss an area that may be a strength of yours but also how that might potentially create a blind spot or challenge for you when working on a team.

USING PEER-TO-PEER OBSERVATIONS FOR COLLABORATING

One way teachers can build competence and resilience is by watching one another teach. Often teachers spend time talking about the craft of teaching or about standards, curriculum, procedures, and routines, but they do not actually take time to watch how those aspects of teaching or instructional techniques are implemented. Creating time and a collective team focus/goal to watch one another teaching is an extremely powerful move. When done well, this can help teachers to reflect on their own practices and support reflective collaborative relationships with those they are observing. Structures and common goals must be in place, including specific purpose or focus area and reflective conversations, for this to work effectively and efficiently.

During team meetings at the beginning of the year or semester, it is important to reflect on a goal for the collaborative group. Once the goal is decided, all efforts should align with that focus. Planning, observations, data collection, and analysis should all be aligned to the team or building goal. For example, if procedures and routines are a major focus for the team/school, then observation rounds should be focused on procedures and routines. While there are many research-based tools to use for observation, such as Charlotte Danielson's Framework for Teaching (Danielson, 2013), this peer-to-peer observation should be extremely focused and simple for teachers to manage. In other words, a simple note catcher or chart that allows teachers to jot down powerful moves they observe and want to reflect upon allows them to focus on the observation instead of the correct way to use a complex note-taking tool. After teachers focus on the powerful moves, they should help to identify one way to support improvement for their colleague in refining their practice. Referencing back to the note catcher/chart to support the conversation after the observation allows for authentic, vulnerable, and reflective conversations between peers (See Table 2.1). The power in these conversations is where we truly get better at getting better.

CONNECTION

You can learn more about setting effective goals in Chapter 6.

TABLE 2.1 ● Sample Powerful Moves Note Catcher

Observation Focus	
Are all students given an opportunity to work on/at the grade-level standard?	
Materials	**Procedures and Routines**
Core text—multiple copies for everyone *Dry erase boards and markers* *Note catcher for vocabulary* *Blank journals for visualizing phrases*	*Students all knew what materials to get out and what was expected in an efficient manner.* *The teacher clearly had set up routines for going over the first read in the text.*
Pedagogy	**Classroom Culture and Mindset**
The teacher provided clear modeling about context clues within informational texts. She provided an opportunity for students to notice the specific types of context clues—like definition and example within the informational text. She then had students practice in pairs before working independently.	*"Thank you Sara for sharing. Would anyone else like to add or share a new hypothesis?"* *A student was late and teacher quickly greeted the learner and got them up to speed.*

Powerful moves are invaluable for student engagement and success in teaching and learning. During this lesson, notate the powerful moves you notice your peer making in each of the categories that follows. Make sure you are looking at this through the lens of your team goal. For example, if the goal is student engagement, notate what the teacher does to support student engagement in these four areas.

After the observation when reflecting with your peers, be prepared to discuss what powerful moves were observed and any wonderings you may have. Discuss why you think specific instructional moves were powerful and what potential impact the moves have on teaching and learning.

CREATING COLLABORATION IN CLASSROOMS

Collaboration extends into the classroom, too. When teachers are mindful and take time to create opportunities for students to work together, students can share their knowledge with one another interchangeably, which motivates them to be more attentive. Purposefully planning the layout of furniture as well as student tasks is also crucial when developing a collaborative classroom culture. For example, putting desks in small cluster groups of four allows students to work in partners more easily versus having desks in rows or isolation. Teachers who facilitate learning or are a "guide on the side" will create a more collaborative culture. In addition, because of diverse cultural backgrounds and varied academic strengths and needs, it has become important for students to work together as they learn the necessary skills of self-governing, inspiring, and honoring one another's viewpoints.

When setting up a collaborative classroom culture, it's necessary to establish norms to make it clear that all students' voices are honored and important. When teachers and students take time to collectively develop and frequently review and adjust classroom norms, it allows for students to grow more cohesive and classroom communication improves.

Students must understand that the goal of the norms is to develop an environment where all students' academic achievement is promoted. Norms should be developed with students; these are not rules presented by the teacher. When facilitating the development of norms, teachers can have students create a Problem-Norm or Sounds Like/Looks Like T-chart depending on the grade level. (See Tables 2.2 and 2.3 for examples.)

Here's how you can cocreate norms to help establish your collaborative classroom:

1. Have students move into partner groups and draw pictures or write about what they think expectations might be for routines. Sample routines can be found in Tables 2.2 and 2.3.

2. Bring students back together and have them share ideas/expectations from one of the routines.

3. Ask the other students if they all agree or have things they might want to add to that specific routine. Create a poster with the agreed-upon expectations to display in the classroom.

4. Leave enough space on the routine poster to add new agreed-upon ideas throughout the year.

5. If students disagree over an item, ask them, "Does the suggestion promote academic growth and achievement for everyone?" This will help students to express their opinions and bring clarity to the routine or norm.

TABLE 2.2 • Sample K–2 Collaboration Sounds Like/Looks Like T-chart

ROUTINE	SOUNDS LIKE	LOOKS LIKE
Working with a partner	Listening to everyone's ideas.	Both partners are collaborating and working together on tasks.
Choosing flexible seating in the classroom for small groups	Students talking and working at a reasonable noise level while staying on task.	Students are choosing responsible spaces to work, even though this could be under a table or in creative space.
Gathering and putting materials away from small group time	Students may be talking, but they are working together to clean things up from their small group.	All students have a responsibility for putting materials away. Students are working as a team, or students have an assigned cleanup job.
Talking and sharing ideas	All participants are taking turns sharing ideas, and everyone's voice is heard and valued.	Sentence stems may be used for sharing ideas. "I agree with this solution because...."
Sharing manipulatives and materials	Learners are kindly asking one another to use materials.	All learners are using manipulatives; one student is not dominating the materials.
Listening to others talk	Students respectfully listen to one another when they are speaking.	One voice at a time is being heard.

(Continued)

(Continued)

ROUTINE	SOUNDS LIKE	LOOKS LIKE
Independent work	Teachers and learners may want to determine if independent work is done quietly or if there is an opportunity for discussion. This may look different depending on the task.	Teachers and students will want to determine how they work best independently. Is this an environment in which students may need privacy, or can they still be sitting in cooperative groups?
Playing with others	Encouraging words would be used instead of hurtful words.	Feet and hands are used respectfully and not to hurt one another.

TABLE 2.3 ● Sample Intermediate Problem-Norm Anchor Chart

AREAS TO REFLECT ON	POTENTIAL PROBLEM	NORM
Communication with peers	Learners interrupt one another.	All voices are valued and listen respectfully while others are speaking.
Equity of voices	Only certain voices are heard.	All learners have an opportunity to contribute to the conversation.
Cell phones	Learners are distracted by phones during direct instruction.	Learners use phones during specific times of the day to respect the learning environment.
Personal items	Students have personal items out that can distract them or others from learning.	There is a specific space where students must keep their own belongings that feels safe. There is a specific time personal items can be used in class.
Different perspectives	Students have a variety of backgrounds and beliefs, which can create tension or biases in a classroom.	All voices are seen, heard, and valued.
Physical workspace	Materials are spread out and not taken care of.	All learners are responsible for taking care of the learning environment.
Intolerance	Biases can create tension, and this may lead to intolerance.	Create a safe space for all to learn and grow academically, socially, and emotionally.
Group work	One student dominates the task, and not all learners are working collaboratively on the assigned group task.	All participants in a group have been given a specific role to assist in the group assignment.
Entering and exiting class	Rowdy behavior exiting a learning environment can get students hurt physically or emotionally.	Clear routines are established for exiting and entering learning environments.
(Space for student ideas)		

Developing norms, setting up furniture in a classroom that fosters teamwork, and creating student tasks that create peer-to-peer discourse takes time. However, these specific moves are powerful when developing a classroom environment that focuses on collaboration, which supports growth for all students in self-governing, inspiring, and honoring one another's viewpoints.

CREATING COLLABORATIVE SCHOOL–HOME CULTURES

Positive family–school relationships are essential for the academic and social-emotional success of students. According to the Institute for Student Achievement,

> The reason for educators and families to cooperate, coordinate and collaborate is to enhance learning opportunities, educational progress, and school success for students. Therefore, family–school interactions focus on what each partner can do to improve the development and learning of children and youth. (Oakes, 2015)

Often students compartmentalize their lives in two separate spaces—their home life and their school life. It is essential to create family–school partnerships that allow students to have connections between the two most important influences in their academic and overall learning.

As you strive to create a collaborative partnership with the families of your students, keep in mind that parents' experiences with school growing up will affect how they interact with you and the other educators in your school building. If a parent experienced something negative in the past, it can create defensive armor or skepticism of their child's current educators. It is essential to recognize that a family's or caregiver's past experiences and attitudes toward school are not necessarily personally aimed at you. Therefore, proactively planning a positive first interaction with parents can help set the student, family, and educator up for success.

CONNECTION

Chapter 4 includes some ideas that will further support communication with families.

In addition to creating positive relationship-building interactions with families, goal setting with families can be a great strategy to build collaboration. When setting goals with students and families, it is important to use language from a non-deficit model while focusing on a student's strengths and growth. Educators can both model this kind of language for families and help to remove any deficit beliefs they may have about a child or family. When setting goals, it is important to highlight areas of strength and areas for opportunity. For example, a statement like, "We need to focus on math," could reinforce a deficit mindset that the student is not good at math. Instead, be more specific and say, "In math, Ellen is showing high achievement with numbers and operations. An area that we need to continue to focus on is measurement and data." This growth mindset goal-setting allows for clear communication and empowers students to know what they can work on at school and at home. It is important to remember parents may need examples of the specific problems that fall in these instructional areas. Breaking down the academic language and giving examples of the academic areas a student either needs support in or has mastered is extremely helpful when communicating with parents. Sharing with families' specific examples of things to practice at home can also start to remove mindsets for families like, "We aren't good at math in our family."

When setting goals, it is important to highlight areas of strength and areas for opportunity.

Brené Brown in her book on communication and leadership says, "Clear is Kind" (Brown, 2018, p. 41). Make sure you bring clarity to each content area. Highlight instructional areas where the student has relative strengths and relative areas for potential focus. Creating a goal and checking in on the progress of the goal monthly with the student and families is a great collaborative strategy that can lead to academic success for students. In addition, celebrating the progress of the goal with families can contribute to a positive family–school connection.

SAMPLE GOAL-SETTING TEMPLATE

Highlight the relative area of strength for each content area. Next identify an area that the teacher, student, and parents plan to support in the upcoming quarter. Determine how the area of need might be supported by each stakeholder.

READING INSTRUCTIONAL AREAS	MATH INSTRUCTIONAL AREAS	SCIENCE INSTRUCTIONAL AREAS
Phonemic awareness (Phonics) Fluency Literature comprehension Information comprehension Vocabulary	(Measurement and data) Fact fluency Number and operations Geometry Algebraic thinking	Earth and space Life science (Physical science)

Identified Goal Area

Identified Goal Area

Identified Goal Area

Informational comprehension

Fact fluency

Earth and space science

Teacher: *Support student in navigating an informational text.*

Student: *Read two informational (nonfiction) texts per week.*

Parents: *Help monitor child reading informational (nonfiction) text. Ask them what they are reading about or learning from the informational text.*

Teacher: *Create/Determine materials to support student in fact fluency. Consider games rather than worksheets, as they are more engaging.*

Student: *Work on multiplication fact fluency at school and home.*

Parents: *Support child at home with materials the teacher provides to increase fact fluency or help to monitor progress.*

Teacher: *Help student find books in the library on Earth and space science. Also, provide links to things like National Geographic Kids for students to self-explore on Earth and space science.*

Student: *Explore books and resources related to the identified goal to build background knowledge.*

Parents: *Help monitor child using resources to learn more about identified area in science. Ask them questions and have discussions about why learning about the Earth or science might be helpful for them in the future.*

The Big Ideas

In this chapter you discovered the importance of collaborating with colleagues, students, and families. In addition, you learned that collaboration and communication are necessary when ensuring that all stakeholders feel seen, valued, and heard. Continue to use the questions and templates from this chapter throughout your year as you incorporate the habit of collaboration into your practice.

As you have conversations with your team, reflect on the importance of building regular interactions with colleagues or mentors, as this is crucial in forming and maintaining lasting relationships. Revisit your team norms as you set up a consistent schedule to meet as a grade-level or content area team. We are better together and must commit to removing barriers to ensure the regular scheduled meetings have a priority for all stakeholders so that we can focus on the habit of collaboration.

Let's Reflect

What were the differences and/or similarities between your current beliefs about collaboration and those you held prior to the COVID-19 pandemic?

_____

_____

_____

What expectations do you hold about working collaboratively with your team? How could those expectations positively or negatively impact your teamwork?

_____

_____

_____

How do you want to foster a collaborative learning environment for your students? What challenges do you still need to contemplate to set up a learning environment for the conditions of success?

_____

_____

_____

What's Next?

In Chapter 3, you will first explore the habit of having high expectations for all stakeholders. Many factors impact high expectations for all. You will investigate how a student's academic identity can be positively or negatively impacted by the expectations set by their educators, family, and peers. As you move through Chapter 3 and the chapters that follow, you will also see a common theme emerging: Communication is essential throughout all the habits of resilient teaching.

Set High Expectations for All

Sydney, an instructional coach, was recently observing and supporting teachers in a PLC (professional learning community). The teachers were aligning grade-level standards and analyzing tasks that students were going to work on to show proficiency in the standard. Teachers were developing scaffolds, differentiation, and enrichment to support their students. However, Sydney noticed that the teachers kept referring to some of the students as "low baby" and "highflyer." The students were being sorted into these differentiated supports, but not all teachers were using evidence to make these decisions.

Based on her observations, Sydney was concerned that the teachers were not using an asset-based mindset and that they might have some blind spots with regards to students' academic readiness levels. Sydney recognized the demanding work the teachers were putting into planning but wanted to ensure teachers were using evidence and a growth mindset not their biases regularly to support kids. She also wanted to ensure that all students would have the opportunity to rumble with high-quality, grade-level tasks.

WHY HIGH EXPECTATIONS MATTER

In the context of education,

> The term high expectations, typically refers to any effort to set the same high educational standards for all students in a class, grade level, school, or

education system. The concept of high expectations is premised on the philosophical and pedagogical belief that a failure to hold all students to high expectations effectively denies them access to a high-quality education, since the educational achievement of students tends to rise or fall in direct relation to the expectations placed upon them. (Great Schools Reform, 2020)

In essence, a student's academic identity can be positively or negatively impacted by the expectations set by their educators, family, and peers. Carol Dweck's research on growth and fixed mindset furthers this point, by showing that even a student's expectation of themself can directly impact their academic achievement. Dweck's research found that,

> Students' mindsets, how they perceive their abilities, played a key role in their motivation and achievement, and we found that if we changed students' mindsets, we could boost their achievement. More precisely, students who believed their intelligence could be developed outperformed those who believed their intelligence was fixed. (Dweck, 2016, p. 1)

Holding high expectations for all students matters on many levels and is a habit that educators must prioritize. In Chapter 1, we started to explore how our language and potential deficit mindset, or inequitable mindset, could negatively impact our colleagues and students. As such, we must approach high expectations for all with mindfulness. As mentioned in Chapter 1, our purpose is not to "fix" our students but provide equitable access to rigorous content while preparing all students to be college and career ready.

WHAT HIGH EXPECTATION MINDSET FOR ALL IS . . .	WHAT HIGH EXPECTATION MINDSET IS NOT . . .
• Believing that all students can learn	• Believing that some students have difficulties and are unable to learn
• Understanding that instructional effort is a pathway to supporting student mastery of standards	• Feeling that instructional effort is fruitless, and the learner is unmotivated and not at grade-level standard because of it
• Understanding that a particular standard or learning intention might need to be broken down more, and it might take more time for students to master	• Believing that a standard or learning intention is too hard for some students because of learning loss
• Embracing the mantra, "I will use a different strategy with my learners."	• Embracing the mantra, "I give up, these students are too low for me to reach."

HOW VERBAL LANGUAGE
AFFECTS HIGH EXPECTATIONS

The power of the words we use and hear can either empower or prohibit us from reaching our highest level of growth and achievement. Consider, for example, how we lean in and listen carefully when we receive feedback from our families, peers, and evaluators. The words they use help us sort out our areas of strength and where we may need support. Sometimes these words (feedback) have been helpful in our learning journey, and other times the messages have deeply wounded us and potentially prevented growth. The same is true with the words and the feedback we use with our students.

There is an old children's nursery rhyme that is completely counterproductive when thinking about the power words/messages have on children; "Sticks and stones may break my bones, but words will never hurt me." Many of us have received the message that words are not supposed to impact us. However, Carol Dweck's research (e.g., 2016) with growth mindset along with Jo Boaler's *Mathematical Mindsets* (e.g., 2015) points out the fact that words/feedback/hidden messages do impact a student's self-efficacy.

Being vulnerable with kids and sharing when you might need to restate something or apologize for how you said something shows students you are a reflective and empathetic teacher.

The more we lean in and rumble with our own academic identity the more mindful we will be when working with the students whose academic growth and achievements we have agreed to support. As adults it is important to spend time reflecting on how someone else's words have either been helpful or hurtful in our own academic identities. The more aware we are of how we have been impacted by other people's verbal language the more mindful we become of how and what we want to communicate with our students.

Spend some time reflecting and using the matrix that follows as you think about your academic identity and how different people (influencers) may have impacted how you think about your academic strengths or areas for growth throughout your life. (See examples in chart.)

SAMPLE ACADEMIC IDENTITY CHART

INFLUENCER	CONTENT AREA	FIXED MINDSET MESSAGE (NEGATIVE FEEDBACK)	GROWTH MINDSET MESSAGE	POTENTIAL IMPACT ON YOUR ACADEMIC IDENTITY
Example: Teacher	Reading: Relative strength is informational texts. Potential area for growth is literature.	None	I can tell you are loving informational texts. It is evident that you use context clues when navigating informational texts. How would you feel setting a goal of using context clues in literature? We could start with visualization and work together on this new goal, or you could choose a type of context clue to practice in literature.	I am a reader, writer, and creative thinker. I can use my strengths from what I know about reading informational texts to help me become better at reading literature.
Example: Teacher	Reading: Relative strength is informational texts. Potential area for growth is literature.	You are struggling with literature and seem unmotivated to read. What are you going to do to change this?	None	I do not like to read and am not very good at it.
Parent				
Teacher				
Peer/Sibling				
Coach or Manager				

"Words are enormously powerful tools that most people do not fully appreciate. Although people recognize the importance of communication skills, they do not necessarily grasp how to become more effective communicators" (Markus, 2023). Typically, teachers who hold high expectations for all students are emotionally responsive and use respectful caring language (Frey & Fisher, 2022). Consider how these phrases can be reworded using growth mindset language that communicates high expectations for all students.

GROWTH MINDSET	FIXED MINDSET
I can learn new things.	I am not good at this; I will stick to what I know.
I recognize what area I need to work on and continue to get better.	This is boring or too hard; I want to work on what I can already do.
I wonder how they got good at that. I want to try to get good at that as well.	It's easy for him/her. They were born smart.
I am inspired by others' success.	I am resentful when others succeed and I don't.
I believe in possibilities.	I don't believe in possibilities and am limited to what I can do or what my circumstances have limited me to doing.

HOW NONVERBAL LANGUAGE AFFECTS HIGH EXPECTATIONS

"In high expectation classrooms, the emotional climate is caring and nonthreatening" (ASCD March 2022). Nonverbal communication has the power to foster or hinder high expectations for all students. This includes facial expression, posture, gestures, breathing, eye contact, and paralanguage—also known as tone. According to Michael Grinder's meta-research on nonverbal communication, 80 to 90 percent of communication is nonverbal (Grinder, 2023). Consider these examples: A heavy sigh might indicate exhaustion or frustration to a group of students or colleagues. Rolling eyes might indicate agreement or disagreement. A gesture or signal can guide or deter students from doing or not doing something. Squinting eyes may indicate frustration or disapproval. A smile may indicate joy or approval.

We must be mindful of how our nonverbal communication can send messages that can help or hurt our students' perception of consistent, high expectations. A teacher who is mindful about nonverbal communication is intentional about developing an emotionally safe climate in their classroom, which directly impacts students' perceptions of expectations.

Students also use nonverbal communication when engaging or disengaging in learning. A student or group of students slouched down in their chairs or laying their heads on the desk may indicate exhaustion, learned helplessness, or boredom. This nonverbal communication should signal the teacher to change up a routine or try a strategy to help re-engage the students. Having strategies that allow students to stand up and move around the room while engaging in student discourse will help them to respond more efficiently when nonverbal signals are present. Students might sigh if they are not thrilled about a learning task they are about to engage in. A student giving a presentation may look down at their feet, which may indicate low self-esteem. Making sure you notice and respond to your students' nonverbal communication is just as important as monitoring your own. Watching nonverbal communication among students can also help a teacher monitor bullying. When we are noticing and responding to these nonverbal interactions, we are creating a caring emotional climate that supports high expectations for all students.

Reflect and use the graphic organizer to describe ways you have noticed nonverbal communication impacting high expectations.

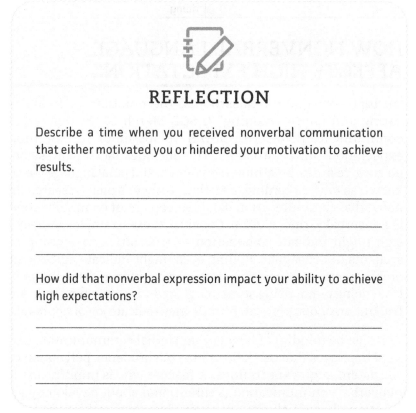

REFLECTION

Describe a time when you received nonverbal communication that either motivated you or hindered your motivation to achieve results.

_____

_____

_____

How did that nonverbal expression impact your ability to achieve high expectations?

_____

_____

_____

What area of nonverbal communication do you want to intentionally focus on in your communication moving forward?

_____

_____

_____

HOW HIGH EXPECTATIONS AFFECT LESSON PLANNING AND ANALYZING DATA

Think about how you planned for a recent vacation. Before jumping in the car/airplane chances are you spent a significant amount of time planning and preparing for your adventure. You may have spent time reflecting on whether the vacation would be at a beach, a mountain, a desert; the sights and sounds of a city; or time spent with family. Next, you may have investigated the area you plan to explore and decided on activities to do once you arrive. If you were traveling with friends or family, it likely required complex preparation because you were navigating the needs of many individuals as you set off on your adventure. You may have needed different items (varied sizes of clothes, snacks, medications, genres of books) for the travelers. Prior to the vacation, you may have also analyzed the weather. The closer you got to your vacation the more frequently you likely checked the weather app on your phone to help determine any last-minute changes that may occur. Finally, you packed your suitcase(s) accordingly, and away you went.

Creating a unit or module of study for your students is a remarkably similar process to planning for a vacation. It is necessary to look at the student learning intentions, success criteria, resources, and formative and summative assessments prior to "the plane taking off." Casually looking over the student learning intentions and summative assessment a few days before administering it is like getting on a plane and not really knowing what destination you are headed off to. Furthermore, it would be important to know how the students' past experiences with travel might impact them emotionally. Does the idea of going on a trip bring anxiety or excitement to the student? This type of instructional planning—or lack thereof—inevitably fails to hold high expectations for all students.

To truly hold high expectations for all students, teachers need to carefully plan for instruction and know where their students need to end up prior to teaching a new unit or module. This type of planning is called "backward planning design." In the past, starting with the first lesson in a module and working chronologically through a resource or curriculum was the practice expected for teachers and students. At the end of the unit, students typically took a summative test based on the curriculum. However, this practice did not yield high expectations for all nor the growth and achievement results desired because it focused on chronological delivery of instruction without considering scaffolds and/or enrichments that may have been needed to reach the diverse needs of all learners. Using the backward planning design allows teachers to clearly determine the destination that they need all students to get to. This allows teachers to understand how they will need to prepare for lessons as they have high expectations for all students to reach the learning objective or grade level "destination."

As part of the backward planning design process, formative assessments and learning-focused feedback need to be strategically embedded into instruction so that students know what learning intentions they are doing well in and what support or purposeful practice they might need within a specific standard. Learning-focused feedback throughout a unit of study can also bridge gaps in student learning and support student growth and achievement in grade-level standards. To help ensure high expectations for each learner are maintained throughout a unit of study, there are three essential questions that a teacher should ask:

1. Where is the learner going?

2. Where is the learner now?

3. What's next in the learning journey for each student?

In order to answer these questions fully, it is essential to gather and use/analyze evidence or data. This data can then help inform decisions about how to plan for scaffolds, differentiation, and enrichment within a unit of study. Often, we have blind spots about our students' ability to navigate various instructional areas/clusters of standards, and it is important to recognize the role data has in planning for instruction. When we plan with high expectations for all in mind, we must intentionally analyze evidence such as student work, pretests, or other formative assessments to more definitely understand what our students might or might not be instructionally ready for learning.

FIGURE 3.1 ● Formative Assessment Cycle

Where is the learner GOING?

CLARIFYING LEARNING

Engage learners to understand what they're learning, why they're learning, and what constitutes success

Where is the learner NOW?

ELICITING + ANALYZING EVIDENCE

Employ multiple methods to gather evidence of each learner's thinking to inform next steps in the learning

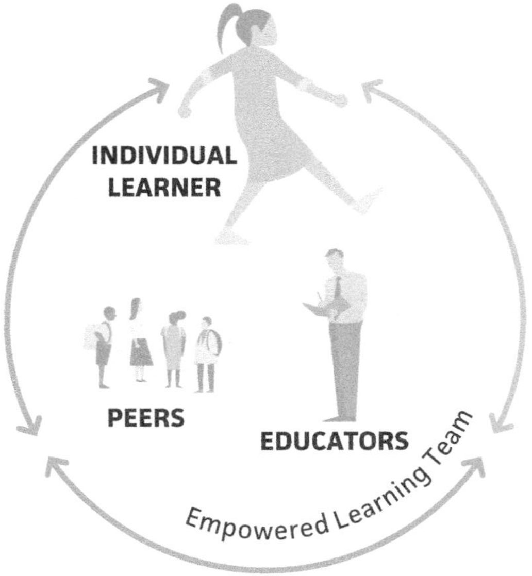

PROVIDING ACTIONABLE FEEDBACK

Use learning-focused feedback to move learners forward

WHAT'S NEXT in the learning journey?

ACTIVATING LEARNERS

Empower learners to be instructional resources for themselves and others

INDIVIDUAL LEARNER

PEERS

EDUCATORS

Empowered Learning Team

Recently, we encountered an example of how analyzing data can directly support instructional planning and uncover unintentional blind spots and assumptions about student readiness levels. While working with teachers in a PLC (professional learning community) to plan for an upcoming informational unit, we analyzed instructional areas in their formative assessments. Teachers were surprised at how well students had done in the instructional area of informational texts. The team had just completed a literature module with students and was starting to determine who would need support with the informational module based off their experience with the literature unit rather than their assessment data. When the team paused and gave themselves permission to look over some formative assessments in conjunction with their MAP data, they were pleasantly surprised at how differently kids performed when it came to the informational standards versus the literature standards. Thus, they realized their students were performing at a higher level with this cluster of standards and planned accordingly rather than unintentionally letting their bias and assumptions about student readiness from the previous unit of instruction potentially contribute to over-scaffolding and lower expectations for their students. When we pause and analyze the formative or summative assessment and use this evidence intentionally, we foster a proactive approach for supporting each student's success.

Use the chart that follows to reflect on how your unintentional blind spots or biases have affected your instruction in the past. Also reflect on how you could use evidence and data more effectively when planning for high expectations for all students in the future.

REFLECTION

What hidden messages have you received from differentiated supports in the past? Were you given enrichment or scaffolds, and how did that impact your mindset?

_____

_____

_____

What evidence do you currently use to make instructional decisions for your entire class?

_____

_____

_____

What evidence do you currently use to make instructional decisions for individual students?

_____

_____

_____

What changes do you want to make when planning for an upcoming unit of learning?

_____

_____

_____

The Big Ideas

In this chapter, we defined what high expectations for all learners are and why this crucial habit is important when working with diverse populations of students. The habit of developing high expectations for all learners is impacted by a variety of factors, as we outlined in this chapter, and needs mindfulness when planning and delivering instruction. We must grapple with the potential hidden messages our body language, tone, and nonverbal communication sends to our students, as well as bring constant mindfulness and reflection to our verbal communication both in one-on-one situations and small or large group settings. Being vulnerable with kids and sharing when you might need to restate something or apologize for how you said something shows students you are a reflective and empathetic teacher.

Finally, in this chapter we defined the role backward planning design has on high expectations for all learners. Knowing where the learners need to go and strategically planning for the learning journey allows teachers to consider how they are supporting all students in accessing the learning goals while using evidence to chart their course.

Let's Reflect

Reflect on your own academic identity. What new learning do you have about the impact verbal and nonverbal communication has had on your own mindset?

_____

_____

_____

When thinking about verbal and nonverbal communication, what area do you think you want to grow in?

_____

_____

_____

What is your current practice for using data to impact planning for all learners? What would you like to change?

_____

_____

_____

What's Next?

In Chapter 4, we will think about diverse types of data and how to use the evidence to drive instruction. In addition, we will reflect on and define why an equitable approach for using data is important, as well as dig deeper into the relationship it has to the habit of high expectations for all learners. Get ready to investigate how using data to drive decisions illuminates bias in our decision-making that may inadvertently influence how effectively we are upholding rigorous expectations for instruction.

CHAPTER 4

Use Data to Drive Decisions

As Oscar, a high school math teacher, sat down at his desk, he stared at the pile of papers on his desk and began organizing them into groups. Within a short time, he realized he had five different samples of student learning evidence from the week. Each paper told a story, and it was time to explore the data. He began to transfer the resulting scores of one particular assessment into the online grading platform used at his school. He smiled to himself as he noticed upon finishing that a substantial portion of the class now had overall grades in the range of 80 to 90 percent. His thoughts drifted to another data source he needed to gather—a separate record of which students had not completed recent assessments and learning tasks. Next, he shifted to the data-tracking tool his PLC (professional learning community) used to enter yet a different dataset in preparation for his grade-level meeting: the percentage of students who correctly solved specific quadratic equation questions across each different learning task. To his surprise, these numbers suggested that less than half the class could adequately show proficiency on the standard of focus from last week's instruction. His earlier smile faded, and he began to realize the conflicting information across his data sources, but where to begin resolving the issues?

WHY DATA SHOULD GUIDE OUR DECISIONS

In Chapter 3, you began exploring the critical reasons why data must guide our daily work as educators. You likely connected your personal experience to the reality that, at any given moment, the amount of data available to you as a teacher may rival that of a research practitioner. Attendance reports, daily formative assessments, behavior logs, exit tickets, and the list goes on. Yet unlike a research scientist, the skill of analyzing, interpreting, and synthesizing data into useful information through an efficient, straightforward process may have only been a small fraction of the training required to become a classroom teacher. When paired with the quantity of decisions teachers find themselves facing on a daily, even hourly, basis, data can empower teachers to become masters of highly effective instruction and extraordinarily efficient users of a most precious resource: time. Data, in short, should fuel teachers' work like carbohydrates fuel an endurance athlete. As such, teachers deserve to develop expertise in knowing which data to utilize, when to apply it, and how to embrace data as a constant partner in guiding efforts to cultivate student learning.

CONNECTION

Chapter 8 describes how to prioritize information efficiently and make informed decisions to positively effect instruction.

Too often, we find ourselves urged to make an important decision or to justify an assumption using singular data points or using misaligned data for the given problem. As Oscar experienced in the preceding example, data can be daunting or even downright confusing at times. When we gather data without beginning our process with a specific question or problem we aim to address, it's possible to make judgments or decisions that are disconnected to our intended goal. Oscar, for instance, gathered an immense amount of student-learning evidence—all great sources of data. However, the data answered distinct questions:

- What was the average student performance across evidence sources?

- What students did not yet produce evidence of learning?

- What did students know and understand about the specific standard related to solving quadratic equations from the prior week's instruction?

Imagine if Oscar had initiated the process of scoring and reviewing the results of his students' learning tasks with a clear question about student understanding of the standard on quadratic equations. He would have been able to make decisions that inform his next instructional moves more effectively and with greater impact.

Data is a crucial driver for making decisions of every type, whether significant or small. It's normal to approach our everyday decisions based on emotion (trusting our "gut"), personal experience, or even guesswork! Gathering and using a set of data, however, provides an effective antidote to subjectivity in feedback cycles such as those described in Chapter 7, for example. When seeking to offer a fellow teacher feedback on their efforts to increase student engagement, our opinions may be fraught with emotional triggers, whereas data provides factual, objective evidence of observations that become actionable feedback sources. Collecting the numbers of students who are actively engaged in a learning task or documenting the amount of time that the teacher is speaking versus the students are speaking about the activity presents explicit evidence—a dataset—that removes any opinion and offers a clear measure of progress or a starting point for improvement efforts.

Becoming comfortable with knowing what purpose data serves, what data to collect for different situations, and how to use it in your own individual pursuits as well as collaborative ventures takes time. Making a habit, or routine, of regularly practicing the strategies in this chapter will build your confidence toward becoming a master of data-driven decisions! For the utmost benefit in applying these practices, be sure to utilize them in tandem with those you find in other chapters.

EFFECTIVE DATA USE IS . . .	EFFECTIVE DATA USE IS NOT . . .
• Appropriately simple, relevant and meaningful to the teacher	• Vast and complex in nature
• Grounded in learning goals or expectations	• Disconnected from learning goals
• Done regularly and for various purposes	• Only done to evaluate completed activities, assessments, or actions (i.e., summative in nature)
• Grounded in curiosity and inquiry	• Based on affirming an assumption or to perpetuate a personal belief
• Done collaboratively with appropriate structures for group work	• Done in a "vacuum" (i.e., always alone or without ever sharing findings or interpretations)

MAKING DATA USE A HABIT

For data to effectively inform a teacher's decisions about anything but, most importantly, student learning, there must be processes in place to make meaning from the information. Data becomes rich, purposeful information that paints a picture or tells a story when individuals or groups construct new understandings and connect prior knowledge to the patterns that emerge. "Learning occurs when we shift from professional certainty to conscious curiosity" (Wellman & Lipton, 2017). By embracing an open mind and constantly endeavoring to uncover new information that empowers our ability to make effective decisions, we move from seeking data as if we were on a witch hunt to collecting data as if we were on a treasure hunt!

Intentionally collecting data becomes a habit in response to the presence of a question or problem. Sometimes it can feel as though we collect data simply for the fact of saying we gather the information, but there isn't a clear purpose in place yet. In fact, it's far too easy to jump to the "response" or "action" stage when confronted with data rather than beginning with inquiry and intentionally seeking to understand the problem. Our understanding can only emerge from thoughtful examination of the evidence in front of us, and to ensure effective action steps are designed, this examination cannot be skipped. Engage in the cycle of inquiry. Ask, *what? why? when?* and identify the data that may answer the questions.

CONNECTION

Use the activities in this chapter to guide your data-gathering practices and visit the strategies for effective prioritization in Chapter 8 to help you efficiently use your time.

Regularly engaging with data of any kind can become a routine that leverages your expertise around instruction in new ways. In order to develop your own "data habits," start by keeping them simple and convenient. Noticing that you may have been basing important decisions on "hunches," or assumptions, will create awareness around new solutions to problems or answers to questions as you gather and utilize facts or evidence—data—to reframe your thinking processes and choose action steps or pathways that get you where you want to be! Data use will become a habit of practice that grounds your efforts in navigating the complexities of constant change and uncertainty.

REFLECTION

PERSONAL DATA INVENTORY: PRE-LEARNING ACTIVITY

What types of data do you currently gather as a teacher (student learning data, attendance, etc.)?

_____

_____

_____

When do you typically gather each of these different data types?

_____

_____

_____

Why do you gather each of these different types of data?

_____

_____

_____

What are some examples of how the data you gather has influenced a change in your teaching practice in some way?

_____

_____

_____

GETTING TO KNOW THE DIFFERENT TYPES OF DATA

The first step toward becoming a confident user of data to drive your decision-making is to understand what types of data you might gather as a classroom teacher. Data is not relegated to student assessment results. Different data sources may serve a different purpose or may merit being used in conjunction with other data sources during analysis. We can seek data—or evidence—to certify student learning and to inform next actions to take in our instruction. Or perhaps we gather evidence of behavior patterns in conjunction with parent survey results to determine a response that incorporates all possible context in our decision-making. A sample of different sources is shown in the chart that follows.

DATA SOURCE	PURPOSE
Attendance records	Identify missed learning opportunities for specific students
Observations during performance tasks	Certify student learning; understand student social-emotional development
Empathy interviews	Determine student readiness for instruction; incorporate learner context into planning (see strategies in next section)
Learning evidence (formative or summative assessments, projects, etc.)	Certify student learning following instruction; inform planning for future instruction
Individual conversations with students	Gain insight into language processing abilities; gain evidence of student understanding
Feedback surveys	Understand student perceptions of the learning environment and individual learner needs

HOW TO CHOOSE WHAT DATA TO COLLECT AND WHEN

When beginning the data collection process, it's easy to get buried in all of the many pieces of information at your fingertips on any given school day. Before engaging in the collection of data with intention, begin with purpose. What is the question you are interested in answering or the problem you are trying to solve? When focusing your data collection around student learning of standards, for example, an excellent place to begin determining what question you intend to answer or problem you aim to solve is by visiting the success criteria established for a lesson or unit of instruction. By using a variety of processes and tools to collect goal-aligned learning evidence, you ensure your efforts will provide you with information and ideas that center around the purpose already established for your instructional plans to move student learning forward.

Consider this example: In a third-grade classroom, recent assessment results suggest that students are struggling with the learning goal of connecting textual evidence to inferences. Following is the problem statement:

> **Problem statement:** *Third-grade students demonstrate difficulty with connecting textual evidence to inferences.*

Now, this problem statement is currently lacking a key element: data. It's possible the statement is a generalization, a "hunch," or an assumption that requires validation to ensure it can be addressed effectively in the classroom. The next question becomes, What data will allow us to respond to the problem? In this instance, some examples of data sources could include student writing samples, classroom formative assessments, or individual conversations with students. Using your professional judgement, you're ready to determine the type and quantity of data sources that will give you a complete understanding of student learning related to this example problem statement.

Use the table that follows to practice identifying a problem statement or question, then identify all of the possible data sources you could potentially gather to address it.

REFLECTION

A recent observation I have about a student or my class is:

_____

_____

_____

Convert the observation into a problem statement.

_____

_____

_____

The data sources I might gather to address the problem statement include the following:

_____

_____

_____

Use the next reflection box to practice connecting your data collection, your problem statement, and the success criteria for a lesson or unit of instruction:

REFLECTION

A success criteria for this lesson/unit is the following:

_____

_____

_____

A source of learning evidence I have gathered thus far suggests that student progress toward the success criteria is:

_____

_____

_____

The problem I need to address or question I want to answer is now the following:

_____

_____

_____

Additional data that might further inform student progress toward the success criteria includes the following:

_____

_____

_____

These processes may be very new to you, or perhaps they are routines already embedded in your practice. We recommend practicing these processes often until they become very comfortable—almost second nature—just like a habit!

BUST BIASES WITH EVIDENCE, NOT ASSUMPTIONS

Analyzing or interpreting data is inherently at risk for influence by our personal identities, biases, or prior knowledge and experiences. These examples could potentially feel familiar to you: A teacher who has worked in a school for several years has developed beliefs around the characteristics of *typical* students in the school, which inadvertently informs their judgments of all students. Or an educator who had very positive experiences in school growing up does not really understand how students' attitudes toward school could be influenced by negative prior experiences and thus misjudges students as being "lazy" or "disruptive" when they don't engage according to his or her expectation. Understanding our personal identities, biases, and prior knowledge/experience is important when we consider the kinds of statements we make in the data gathering and interpretation process. We might generalize a student as being "bad at math" when in fact we aren't considering the vast context surrounding their mathematical learning nor the highly nuanced skills and concepts they do, in fact, understand. A simple practice to develop our objectivity and mitigate biased statements is to practice changing our statements from *assumption* to *evidence*. Practice on the chart that follows to get started.

STATEMENT	EVIDENCE	ASSUMPTION
Some students had difficulty staying engaged.		
The students didn't understand the objective of the activity.		
Two students did not complete the writing sample in class.		
The boys in the class were all completely distracted.		
Fourteen of sixteen students met the success criteria on Tuesday.		
Those students are never in class.		
All but three students incorrectly answered the analysis question on the test.		

*Refer to the Answer Key at the end of the chapter to verify your answers!

COLLABORATIVE INQUIRY CYCLES

As you continue to learn the skills and practices that support impactful collaboration from Chapter 2, you can take your new talents to the next level by bringing data to the conversations!

When you determine a problem to address as a team—whether you are a PLC, a department, a coach–teacher pair, or any other group of educators seeking to improve student learning outcomes—employ a collaborative inquiry cycle together to guide your data conversations. A collaborative inquiry cycle is a four-step process to approach student data of any kind (academic, behavioral, etc.). The collaborative inquiry cycle provides a structure to the conversations in order to maximize opportunities for insights and outcomes. The process includes the following:

1. Powerful predictions
2. Purposeful observations and exploration
3. Thoughtful explanations
4. Measured action

(Adapted from NWEA [n.d.])

For deeper learning on data analysis cycles, be sure to read Bruce Wellman and Laura Lipton's *Data Driven Dialogue: A Facilitator's Guide to Collaborative Inquiry*, MiraVia, 2017.

1. **Powerful predictions:** Before you look at the gathered data, it is important to activate your prior knowledge, make predictions, and bring to the surface any assumptions you may have. Address the question: What do you think we will see in the data? By addressing your predictions prior to analyzing the data, you are preparing for the following opportunities:

   - Illuminate assumptions and biases
   - Create anticipation and curiosity
   - Focus questions we are asking
   - Prepare to grapple with the data

BEGIN STATEMENTS WITH . . .	AVOID . . .
I wonder . . .	Causes
I predict . . .	Explanations
I assume . . .	Ideas for fixing
I expect to see . . .	If only . . .

2. **Purposeful observations and exploration:** In this phase, you are looking to understand the story that the data is telling by focusing on the facts using numerical information rather than letting opinion-based language or assumptions drive your conclusions. Address the question: What do

we actually see in the data? Starting here enhances the objectivity of your approach to the data by requiring ample observation before making assumptions.

- Engage in intellectual "hang time" (allowing for ample silent processing before jumping to solutions)
- Explore multiple storylines/explanations in the data
- Consider data through multiple perspectives
- Avoid "why" and "because"

BEGIN STATEMENTS WITH . . .	AVOID . . .
I see that . . .	Because . . .
I can count . . .	However . . .
Some patterns/trends are . . .	Broad terms (all, most, etc.)
I'm surprised . . .	

3. **Thoughtful explanations:** During this phase, you are analyzing the data to generate multiple theories of causation. Through this process, you are working to prioritize, explain, dig deeper, and identify additional data that may need to be gathered. Address the question: What are we going to act upon?

QUESTIONS TO ASK . . .
What are some possible . . . ?
What are your hunches about?
What do we know about previous attempts to . . . ?
What does past history say about this?
What additional data might help explain?

4. **Measured action:** In the final phase, it is important to convert problem statements into goals and develop an action plan. Address the question: What actions are we going to take? Your action plan should include the following:

- Set clear outcomes
- Identify measurable success criteria
- Articulate necessary action steps
- Implement data-driven monitoring systems

What specifically do we want to accomplish?

What could we do about this problem statement?

What will we do and by when?

What will be different as a result of working on this area?

How can we make the goal measurable so that we know when we achieve it?

What step could we take this week that would move us toward our goal?

Many educators find themselves working with data alone—perhaps your department or grade level are very small, for example. While these activities center around group work, they are perfectly applicable to individual practice! If you find yourself curious about others' perspectives on your findings or want to try these activities in a group, look to Chapter 7 for ideas on finding networks of educators or peer groups to work with!

By integrating collaboration skills from Chapter 2 into your collaborative data conversations, you will elevate the benefits from the collective expertise across each individual at the table. The ability to work effectively together—to become a high-performing group—takes time and demands intentional efforts around developing relationships in equal measure to skills in interpreting data. By utilizing this structured protocol, you are taking another important step on the journey toward becoming skilled and confident at using data to move student learning forward.

GATHERING LEARNER CONTEXT AS A RESPONSIVE DATA PRACTICE

While many sources of data you gather will be directly related to student-learning outcomes, as we strive to fuel both learning success *and* student wellbeing, there are immense opportunities to gather and use learner context information at all stages of the teaching and learning cycle. Dr. Erin Beard, a program director and teaching and learning specialist in Oregon, described learner context in an interview as being comprised of

> the cognitive, social, emotional, behavioral, and physical factors that contribute to a students' overall well-being. Learner context is derived from students' strengths, interests, identities, and funds of knowledge, which also encompass their lived experiences, cultural assets, and prior knowledge. (personal correspondence).

One strategy for gathering and using learner context as you plan instruction might be an empathy interview. Nelsestuen and Smith (2020, p. 59) define empathy interviews as "one-on-one conversations that use open-ended questions to elicit stories about specific experiences that help uncover unacknowledged needs." Once you identify the focus of your interviews (getting to know students at the start of the year or understanding students' experiences in virtual learning, for example), a typical empathy interview protocol has four to eight open-ended, story-based questions developed using stems such as the following:

- Tell me about a time when . . .
- Tell me about the last time you . . .
- What are your best/worst experiences with _____?
- Can you share a story that would help me understand more about . . . ?

Consider the example of using an empathy interview by Rebecca, an 8th grade English teacher:

Toward the end of the school year, my eighth-grade students and I were tired and grumpy! Students were ready to move on to high school. It is always harder at this time for me to engage students in large goals, such as content standards, which can cause stress, frustration, and burn-out for students and me. I used the empathy interview protocol to reveal valuable insights about their ideas, knowledge, and worries. I then applied their insights when planning lessons for the unit of study. This was a way that the students and I could get fresh engagement ideas as well as address worries in real time, which helped decrease feelings of distress. To conduct the empathy interview, I polled my students before, during, and after the unit of study by asking three quick, repeated questions about their sense of success, engagement, and stress related to our unit of study for the large goal. I also answered the questions for myself. Then the students and I examined the data together to notice any patterns and responded accordingly. I adjusted my thinking to make sure I stayed asset-oriented, which more accurately informed how to nurture safe learning spaces and supportive partnerships through the end-of-year challenges. Students felt seen, heard, and valued. They also felt respected, which increased engagement and learning success, including their wellbeing. Plus, I didn't feel like I had to shoulder all the hard work alone, which fueled my success and wellbeing. The reinvestment of time into this plan prevented issues that I'd experienced during the spring in previous years, such as angry tears, unengaged students, and stressed-out teachers, parents, and caregivers.

REFLECTION

Based on the information shared in the example, respond to the questions that follow.

What are the positive impacts of gathering learner context as a form of data to inform your work as a teacher?

_____

_____

_____

How does this concept connect with what you already do with students?

_____

_____

_____

What is one idea you could try next with your students?

_____

_____

_____

ENGAGING STUDENTS IN COLLECTING LEARNING EVIDENCE

When collecting data, or evidence, Dr. Beard also shares that it's very easy to fall into the routine of "learner manager" (a teacher who conducts the gathering of data for their own analysis and use in determining next steps for the class full of individual learners).

As you strive to build students' self-direction, ownership of their learning, and empowerment to engage in their own journey toward mastery, recognize that there are tremendous opportunities in inviting students to be active participants in the collection of their own learning evidence!

As we mentioned earlier, effective data collection is premised upon using a variety of processes and tools to collect evidence aligned to learning goals. Learning goals, or success criteria, should be actively shared with students at every opportunity, and thus your students will be naturally situated to join the evidence-collecting journey. Within your efforts to gather data, consider how you might apply steps to students in these examples.

TEACHER GATHERS . . .	STUDENTS GATHER AND SHARE . . .
Student interviews over learning progress using recent writing samples	Evidence of progress around specific skills between first draft and final draft using teacher-provided rubric
Running records of foundational reading skills	Sticker charts as they master sight words and share progress in parent conferences
Assessment of learning targets measured in an oral presentation	Peer feedback surveys around their oral presentation, synthesized and described in a journal
Math test results	Video recording of themselves narrating how they corrected errors on a recent math test
Student behavior logs tied to a student's IEP goals	Weekly binders tracking daily emotions and sharing why different experiences caused those emotions with a teacher

Using these examples as a guide, develop ideas in the chart that follows for how you might engage students in the process of collecting learning evidence in your own classroom.

REFLECTION

DATA PURPOSE	I WILL GATHER . . .	STUDENTS COULD GATHER . . .

The Big Ideas

In Chapter 3, you examined the critical importance of establishing and upholding high expectations for yourself and for each and every one of your students. Within this chapter, you have learned how to utilize data to drive decisions and have seen how data can illuminate bias in our decision-making that may inadvertently influence how effectively we are upholding rigorous expectations for instruction. Further, you learned strategies for engaging in collaborative inquiry cycles and how to incorporate responsive teaching and learning practices in your daily work. Revisiting this chapter often will catalyze your ability to apply your learning throughout the rest of this book, and it has been situated early in the book for just that reason. Data is not isolated to information about student learning. Rather, data is an invaluable way to clarify your efforts to improve your assessment design following feedback cycles from an instructional coach, as one example. Data can even enable you to monitor how you spend your time. You'll learn more about this data collection technique in the "job crafting" portion of Chapter 10. In short, take advantage of the opportunity for data use to transcend each personal and professional habit described in this book!

Let's Reflect

What will likely be the most significant challenge to your growth in using data skillfully? What actions will you take to overcome that challenge?

_____

_____

_____

What strategies within this chapter are you most excited to implement in your classroom right away? What are you expecting to learn from these first attempts?

_____

_____

_____

What are several urgent questions you have around your students' learning progress this year that you now understand could be addressed with new types of data?

_____

_____

_____

What's Next?

In Chapter 5, you will dive deeply into using procedures and routines to elevate the impact of your teaching practice in every lesson, every day. Though perhaps seemingly simple, developing and applying strategic routines and procedures is an art form that can dramatically influence your confidence and success, as well as the confidence and success of your students, throughout the school year. You'll learn ways to integrate these practices across all areas of your teaching.

Evidence Versus Assumption Answer Key

STATEMENT	EVIDENCE	ASSUMPTION
Some students had difficulty staying engaged.		X
The students didn't understand the objective of the activity.		X
Two students did not complete the writing sample in class.	X	
The boys in the class were all completely distracted.		X
Fourteen of sixteen students met the success criteria on Tuesday.	X	
Those students are never in class.		X
All but three students incorrectly answered the analysis question on the test.	X	

CHAPTER 5

Establish Procedures and Routines

Kyle, an elementary teacher, focuses on procedures and routines from the moment he steps into the school building after summer vacation. At the start of the 2021–2022 school year, Kyle reflected on the incoming students he would soon meet. Kyle speculated that most of his students had some school or classroom experience; however, they were still transitioning from online instruction during the COVID-19 pandemic. He believed it was essential to establish clear expectations around routines and procedures with this new group of kids that would quickly become a community of engaged learners. As a result of this purposeful reflection and planning, the kids in room 310 were engaged in learning goals, and a culture of respect and joy filled the classroom atmosphere.

Kyle took several weeks at the beginning of the school year to create the physical environment and set social-emotional and behavioral procedures and routines for his students to set them up for success. For example, he made sure the students knew where to find materials and how to use them. He spent time showing students how to select books out of his class library. He then helped them create and use specific folders that hold students' individualized learning goals for reading. He taught his students how to build stamina in reading and how to respond during student-to-student discourse discussions. In addition, Kyle modeled and shared a variety of fun chants with his students to grab their attention and took the necessary time setting up classroom norms for how the learners would like to communicate with one another. Just like other years, Kyle rumbled with time management when establishing physical and social-emotional procedures and routines. However, he knew if he prioritized clear routines and procedures with his community of learners, they would know what to expect and be able to move smoothly through the academic expectations in the days, weeks, and months ahead regardless of students' previous experience.

THE IMPORTANCE OF ROUTINES AND PROCEDURES

When was the last time you left your classroom and felt like you had enough energy at the end of the day to hang out with friends, go to the gym, manage extracurricular activities, or read a book for fun? The demands of quality instruction, high-stakes assessments, and increasing student behavioral challenges are exhausting. The beginning and end of a school year bring even more challenges and stresses as the mountain of paperwork or deadlines starts to pile up on your desk. You go to leave your classroom, and you cannot find your keys, computer, or the homework you need to grade because of the upheaval from the afternoon lockdown drill. This has left you feeling scattered.

Perhaps the desire to dive into the curriculum on the first day of school creates tension for you because procedures and routines are not prioritized as urgent and important. The expectation or perceived pressure from administrators, colleagues, and parents to jump into teaching standards and academic content creates time management challenges at the beginning of the year. Grade-level teams also put pressure on one another to do specific projects that have great intentions but might take time that is not practical or manageable. However, developing procedures and routines *are* urgent! These are systems you develop and put in place to complete recurring tasks in the classroom. They provide order and can minimize that "scattered and stressed" feeling for both you and your students. They can help to diminish wasted time searching for materials and provide security for students, which can tend to eliminate some of the behavioral challenges that you may be facing. In addition, when students know the routine or procedure, they don't have to spend cognitive focus on the structure/procedure related to the activity—they can focus on the content they need to learn (Capizzi, 2009). Setting up these procedures and routines may take time up front, but in the end, they will help you maximize your own time and energy.

Stated simply, procedures and routines help us to be effective and efficient. Procedures and routines provide predictable processes, which help to decrease time spent on recurring tasks, which, in turn, provides more time for instruction and learning activities. Established routines also help to eliminate confusion for students, which can directly impact stress and anxiety for students and yourself. The more clarity students have about routines and procedures, the more energy can be spent on being productive, creative, and curious about learning tasks. At the end of the day, procedures and routines can also help you preserve your own energy and allow you to have mental clarity as you pack up your bag and race out the door to the gym or social event you have been longing for.

Procedures and routines provide predictable processes, which help to decrease time spent on recurring tasks which, in turn, provides more time for instruction and learning activities.

ROUTINES INSTEAD OF RULES FOR EFFECTIVE, EQUITABLE CLASSROOM MANAGEMENT

When you hear the phrase "classroom management," what comes to mind? If you are like many teachers and administrators, classroom management has been characterized as being all about the rules and expectations you set to maintain order, keep students focused, and prevent distractions from learning. Rules and expectations are an important aspect of classroom management, and yet they are not enough by themselves. A focus exclusively on the rules in classroom management can create an inequitable environment that reinforces disciplinary systems that disproportionately impact students of color (Milner et al., 2019). The ethos of "controlling students" that characterizes some classroom management practices is at direct odds with our goals for equitable and inclusive classrooms. When students are forced to use rule/behavior clip charts or flip behavior cards publicly, for example, this can bring feelings of shame and embarrassment. Often the same kids seem to clip down the behavior chart or flip a behavior card, which creates a negative mindset, and other students can start to label these students as "the naughty kids" or "the behavior problems." Again, it is important to think about proactively creating a classroom culture where students care and respect one another. Talking to kids privately about the choices they are making and getting to the root of the behavior will be more effective for all.

The ethos of "controlling students" that characterizes some classroom management practices is at direct odds with our goals for equitable and inclusive classrooms.

Traditional classroom management strategies may also have limited impacts on student learning. In large-scale analysis of the research on classroom management strategies, their overall impact on student achievement seems weak compared to other classroom practices (J. Hattie, 2021b). This seems surprising given how much attention we pay to classroom management in teacher preparation, professional learning, and our daily and weekly conversations about what goes on in schools. It is easier to understand once we think about the category itself: "Classroom management" contains a whole host of strategies, from the highly effective to the minimally effective. To experience the true potential of classroom management, we must seek out and use those practices that are most impactful for students.

Here, the research is much clearer: The most impactful classroom management strategies focus on students' social-emotional development (Korpershoek et al., 2016). That is where routines come in. Instead of punishing unruly behavior, clear routines promote positive and appropriate behavior by eliminating the guesswork for students (Capizzi, 2009). Establishing clear routines can also free up instructional time by minimizing students' confusion about what they are supposed to be working on (Capizzi, 2009). For example, creating an anchor chart that describes what partner work looks and sounds like and posting it in a central part of the room is highly effective. Asking a student to voluntarily read the anchor chart prior to partner or small-group work as a reminder to the class sets students up for the conditions of success during their partner or small-group work time. Taking that time to set clear expectations can be invaluable as you think about how to meet the increasingly diverse needs of all the learners in a particular classroom.

EFFECTIVE ROUTINES AND MANAGEMENT ARE . . .	EFFECTIVE ROUTINES AND MANAGEMENT ARE NOT . . .
• Establishing clear routines and procedures, with your students and goals in mind	• Relying on students' previous experience or assuming they know "how to behave" in school
• Cocreating class charts to promote appropriate behavior in different areas of the room	• Telling students the classroom rules and expectations without input from the students
• Reinforcing and celebrating kids modeling routines or behaviors	• Calling students out publicly to flip a card or clip down the chart
• Anchor charts with class goals	• Putting kids' names on the board for behavior consequences
• Having students model what a specific routine might look like as a reminder to the rest of the class about agreed upon expectations	• Displaying names of students for poor choices or missing homework
	• Publicly engaging or contending with a student or group of students

When Sandra started teaching at a new school, she was fore-warned that the students in this class were disruptive and difficult to engage. She partnered with her grade-level teammates before the school year started and developed a shared collection of strategies and actions to cultivate clear, consistent expectations with students right from the start. Beginning with the most basic procedures, such as transitioning between classes in an orderly fashion, all the way to guidelines that students would learn to engage in class discussions using the R.A.C.E model (restate the question, answer the question, cite evidence, explain the answer) whether they were in art class or English, the team knew they were investing heavily in long-term gains. When students arrived, teachers dedicated time each day to teaching and practicing various procedures to celebrate successes and promote consistency across each classroom. As the months went on, Sandra reflected that she could not believe this was the class others had warned her about. Challenges came up, for sure, but communicating the fundamentals of "how we operate" as students from day one minimized confusion and uncertainty and enabled everyone to focus on the work at hand—learning!

Routines really are "the foundation of classroom management" (Lester et al., 2017, p. 398). Your students are looking for a structure to support their learning—establishing that structure early and reinforcing it often is key both to keeping students on task and preventing discipline challenges before they happen (Korpershoek et al., 2016). The routines we describe later in this chapter are designed to help build a culture of care (Ellerbrock et al., 2015) in your classroom that helps students see the value they place in learning, believe in themselves as learners, and keep focus on the activities that are going to drive their academic and overall growth.

BALANCING SHARED OWNERSHIP AND DIRECTIVES FOR PROCEDURES AND ROUTINES

There is a delicate balance between establishing safe systems and procedures and providing an opportunity for students to have a collaborative or shared voice in their classroom environment. Some routines, such as health and safety procedures, may need to be established by the administrator or teacher and taught directly, while other routines and procedures can be created with shared ownership and with the students. For example, safety guidelines on how to exit the building during a fire drill, health protocols, or bus safety routines may need to be shared with students more directly. But procedures for classrooms can be cocreated with your students, refined, and practiced fitting the needs of your specific classroom and the children in it.

Providing opportunities for students to collaborate and have a voice creates a collaborative classroom culture where students feel seen, valued, and heard. Think about your own teaching experiences and the directives you have received from school leadership. Sometimes these directives help bring clarity and efficiency to you as a teacher. Yet you may also have experienced times when you wished you had more voice or influence in decisions that were being made for your school and students. When we are given an opportunity to contribute to conversations and decisions ,we often buy in or support those decisions more cooperatively and with more enthusiasm in execution. Your students share those same feelings of wanting to have an influence on classroom routines, procedures, or rules. As we prepare procedures and routines at the start of the year, it is important to think about the impact student voice and choice have on classroom culture. Student-driven procedures allow for students to help provide more voice and choice in how specific routines are implemented. For example, determining specifically how students work on projects in partners, small groups, or independently can help meet the needs of all learners. Some students enjoy working independently, and providing an opportunity for them to choose independent working time can be extremely helpful. On the contrary, some students thrive in partnerships, and providing opportunities for them to have a voice in their partnerships can also be effective.

Providing an opportunity for students to create routines for the classroom can also help to bond the students together while creating a collaborative classroom climate. Here are some ways to involve students in creating classroom procedures and routines:

- Facilitate conversations with students, asking questions—such as, What kind of environment makes you feel safe and respected? or How can cooperating help everyone in the class to achieve learning goals?
- Serve as a "guide on the side" as students share (and discuss) their ideas on classroom routines
- Ask students to help create a set of classroom norms and/or a vision statement

- Allow students to brainstorm ways they can access or share materials, classroom jobs, communication, and student-to-student discourse routines

When collaborating with students on procedures and routines, it is important to think of ways for verbal and nonverbal processing to help in contributing to the conversation. Posting a question to help foster conversations around specific procedures can be helpful. For example, try asking students, "How do you feel about working with a partner or small group?" or "What behaviors and activities help you to work well in a small group?" Students can then create a poster together and present their ideas to the group. After students have brainstormed and shared their posters with the class, the teacher can create an anchor chart supporting the student's statements around partner or small-group work. Spending time establishing student and teacher expectations helps to create clear and kind communication.

Another efficient way to get kids to share their voices and work collectively is having them create a T-chart poster that says correct on one side and incorrect on the other (or shows a smiley face on one side and a sad face on the other). Helping students to identify behaviors they know are helpful or respectful is another way to bring student voices together and create clear expectations for all learners. You could have students brainstorm how to act on the playground at recess by creating a "Correct/Incorrect" anchor chart. This can be done as a whole group or in partners where students create their own chart to share with the larger group.

Highly effective teachers navigate between facilitating, collaborating, and directing in their instructional practices, which includes setting up clear routines and expectations.

PROACTIVE PLANNING FOR ENVIRONMENTAL AND BEHAVIORAL PROCEDURES AND ROUTINES

Alex had been teaching tenth-grade Algebra II for two years when he received feedback from an instructional coach that his students were completely reliant on him for navigating the classroom experience. "What are we doing today?" or "How do you want me to answer this

(Continued)

(Continued)

problem?" were just a few of the interjections that students freely asked, yet Alex never hesitated to assist them with the answer. He found himself constantly addressing individual students, and class time was less focused than he intended. To shift the balance more toward agentive learning for his students, he implemented strategies found in the "flipped classroom" model. He took time to train students on a new routine in which they were expected to view a short instructional video about the day's learning objective prior to class, and the first activity of every period centered around a "Do Now" problem based on the objective. The problem-solving time was expected to be fully independent until Alex signaled the shift to discussion of their processes and results (allowing him time to move and observe student's methods, gain insight into their understanding of the video content, and make subtle instruction adjustments on the spot). Over time, the routine of this procedure mitigated students' dependency on Alex for directions and sent the consistent message "we are learning today!" across his classes.

To prepare for procedures and routines first, create a journal or a list of procedures and routines that have been done or seen in the past. Reflect on what has gone well in the past, or reflect on innovative ideas for how to modify old routines. When creating your list of routines and procedures, consider what is important to you and what potentially you can let go of. For instance, one teacher may have all student work turned into the same bin every week because it helps to feel organized, while another teacher may not care about a bin. Consider your personal needs and the impact these procedures may have on you and the learners. Categorize the list into physical routines and social-emotional routines as you think through all the details of establishing a new community of learners.

Following is a list of more opportunities for reflecting and establishing clear expectations for a physical and social-emotional learning environment that may help when establishing routines and procedures.

Physical Environment Routines and Procedures

- Physical learning space/environment (e.g., arrangement of furniture, bulletin boards, lighting, and technology)
- How to access and share classroom or personal materials
- Safety protocols (e.g., fire and tornado drills and lockdowns)
- Arrival and dismissal routines for pick-up and drop-off, bus, after school programs

- Use of technology: laptops, cell phones, websites, and educational apps
- How to enter and exit the classroom
- Lunchroom and outside breaks or recess
- Classroom cleaning procedures (establishing that you are not the housekeeper is essential)
- Parent-student-teacher communication
- Attendance and absenteeism routines

Social-Emotional/Behavioral Routines and Procedures

- How to use interpersonal skills to share materials collaboratively
- Classroom communication (e.g., teaching kids how to use compassion and respecting one another's voices)
- How to work with a partner or small group
- How to work independently or ask to work independently when needing downtime
- How to be grateful and encourage one another
- How to create positive relationships with parents and guardians
- How to use a kind tone/words versus unkind tone/words
- How to use appropriate volume of voice for the task/activity
- How to recognize and use appropriate nonverbal communication (smile versus rolling eyes)
- Body awareness (for example, feet and hands to yourself)

In addition, it can be useful to collaborate and talk at a grade-level meeting with other educators, prior to the first days of school. This provides great support when thinking about how to create positive classroom cultures. Veteran teachers will have experience with helpful school-specific routines, while newer teachers can bring fresh creative ideas that add to the group, especially when thinking about helping with creating a collective voice in the classroom. Following are some examples of routines that are good to think about at the beginning of the year.

Routines for the Beginning of the Year

- Physical learning space/environment (e.g., arrangement of furniture, bulletin boards, lighting, and technology)
- How to share materials and resources

- Safety protocols (fire, earthquake, and tornado drills as well as lockdowns)
- Arrival and dismissal routines for pick-up and drop-off, bus, after school programs
- How to enter and exit the classroom

ARRANGEMENT OF FURNITURE AND THE LEARNING ENVIRONMENT

Furniture arrangement in a classroom affects the overall learning environment. A few common configurations that may be used include the following: student desks in quads or pairs, desks in semicircle with the teacher table in the center, student tables instead of desks, and desks in rows. See the chart that follows to see the benefits and potential challenges to each arrangement.

FURNITURE ARRANGEMENT	BENEFIT	CHALLENGE
Desks in pairs or quads	• Supports quick access for student discourse • Creates a collaborative culture	• Students can be more talkative • Testing can be challenging (consider using privacy folders)
Desk in semicircle	• Supports a Socratic method or classroom culture • Teacher can easily see all students during whole-group and small-group instruction	• It takes up a large amount of classroom space • It can be harder for learners and teachers to move about the classroom
Desk in rows	• Students are isolated for testing • It is easy to navigate moving around the classroom	• Difficult for student-to-student discourse • Partner work is more difficult • Teacher may have difficulty seeing all students during whole-group and small-group instruction
Tables	• Less furniture to manage • Excellent for small-group work • Easy to navigate movement around the room	• Bins or storage needed for student materials since they do not have their desk to store items • Testing may require privacy folders since students are facing one another

When considering which configuration you want to set up in your classroom, ask yourself these questions that follow.

REFLECTION

How do I want students to be able to interact during learning time?

_____

_____

_____

How can I make each area as accessible as possible to all learners—and to myself as I circulate the room?

_____

_____

_____

Are there any special pieces of furniture that can help accommodate the learning needs of kids with IEPs?

_____

_____

_____

What is the aesthetic I want my students to feel in this classroom? Calm and focused? Energetic buzz? How will the furniture arrangement contribute?

_____

_____

_____

BULLETIN BOARDS AND
THE LEARNING ENVIRONMENT

You may have mixed emotions about creating bulletin boards in your classroom or out in the hall. If designing bulletin boards is a creative outlet for you, great! If not, give yourself permission to rethink how you use this space so that you do not have to change them so frequently. Bulletin boards and anchor charts can be used to help support or remind students of mission statements, important procedures, routines, and much more so it is important to plan for the limited space. Teaching kids to use bulletin boards as resources or tools so they can be independent and agentive is a powerful way to visually support procedures, routines, and standards. Remember that not every space in your room must be covered, but that pieces can be added over the year as newly cocreated classroom tools are made. There is a fine line between cutesy clutter that distracts students and useful pieces that students can use for learning. It is especially important to be mindful of visually over-stimulating your room with things on the walls. Less clutter means more meaningful and powerful tools for kids to use on a daily basis.

Here are examples of bulletin board content that support effective learning environments:

- A student or class gratitude bulletin board can be created once and added to both with and by students all year

- Cocreated classroom norms, routines, and procedures

- Showcase of student work samples, with reference to *why* they are on the showcase (significant improvement, exemplary examples, etc.)

- Group discussion protocols

- Culture-building or identity-affirming artifacts, such as students' nationalities, recent travel photos, or personal accomplishments

- Class goals toward specific learning objectives or social-emotional development

How might you use bulletin boards and wall space to foster both routines and habits that support social-emotional development? Consider the idea of a gratitude bulletin board or even a jar for kids to hang or drop notes into as they practice sharing about classmates that they are grateful for. When using a bulletin board, students can add a tag to the gratitude wall and periodically share some of the things that have been "captured" as a class. Such routines are simple, and yet they can have such an incredible effect on students' attitudes toward others and on their own self-efficacy.

Walking through classrooms of your teammates or other teachers at your school may also give you some creative ideas for displaying visual supports that reinforce classroom routines and procedures. Just remember, when looking at other classrooms, give yourself permission to find bulletin boards that support procedures and routines. They do not all have to be Pinterest-worthy masterpieces!

When designing your wall space and bulletin boards consider the following questions.

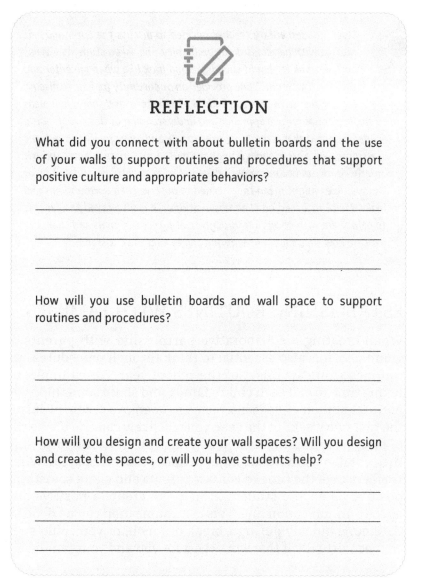

REFLECTION

What did you connect with about bulletin boards and the use of your walls to support routines and procedures that support positive culture and appropriate behaviors?

_____

_____

_____

How will you use bulletin boards and wall space to support routines and procedures?

_____

_____

_____

How will you design and create your wall spaces? Will you design and create the spaces, or will you have students help?

_____

_____

_____

ENTERING AND EXITING THE CLASSROOM

As an educator, you have likely seen students storming through the halls and disrupting classroom or school tranquility, and you will likely have witnessed students walking in a single-file line looking stoic. Often schools will have some schoolwide hall expectations so that the environment is conducive to learning for all. However, it is also important to think about what it looks and sounds like for kids to enter and exit their own classroom. There is a delicate balance between letting kids be disruptive and allowing time for them to have conversations as they line up and prepare to leave the classroom.

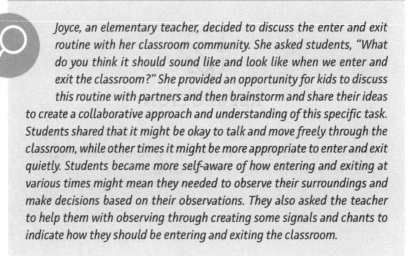

Joyce, an elementary teacher, decided to discuss the enter and exit routine with her classroom community. She asked students, "What do you think it should sound like and look like when we enter and exit the classroom?" She provided an opportunity for kids to discuss this routine with partners and then brainstorm and share their ideas to create a collaborative approach and understanding of this specific task. Students shared that it might be okay to talk and move freely through the classroom, while other times it might be more appropriate to enter and exit quietly. Students became more self-aware of how entering and exiting at various times might mean they needed to observe their surroundings and make decisions based on their observations. They also asked the teacher to help them with observing through creating some signals and chants to indicate how they should be entering and exiting the classroom.

ESTABLISHING ROUTINES WITH FAMILIES

When creating a collaborative partnership with parents or guardians, it is also essential to think through procedures and routines from the onset of the school year. For example, by taking time to call each child's family and share something you notice that their child is interested in or enjoys at school during the first two weeks of the year, you will likely capture the hearts of most of your families and demonstrate your investment in their child's positive-learning experience that school year. When teachers take the time to contact parents and share something positive about the student, it helps to create a positive and open communication line. This communication can be done on the phone quickly during a break or lunch, or you could even connect virtually if that works best for you and your families.

Wade recognized and valued having a positive relationship with his students' families. During the first few weeks of the new school year, he called his students' parents to introduce himself and then purposely shared something he noticed the students were interested in. Wade wanted his students and families to know he was taking an interest in them and noticed each student was a unique individual. Wade said that it was always rewarding and worth the time spent up front connecting with each student's family. He found the routine that worked best for him was to make one to two calls per day. Wade recognized that making a positive connection at the beginning of the year could be helpful, especially if you end up having to communicate with the family for behavior or academic concerns later in the school year.

Often, families are conditioned to only hear from school when something is wrong. Spending time emailing or making a personal call and connection can be one routine you may choose to do throughout the year. Sharing and celebrating academic or behavioral success with a parent can be a simple and rewarding routine. Keep a list of caregivers' phone numbers and emails handy, and work in a time each day to make one to two calls or send one to two emails.

Other examples of routines that help to build collaborative relationships with parents might be the following:

- Provide course outline at the beginning and end of the grading period
- Send weekly or monthly family emails
- Establish and communicate protocols for parents to reach out to teachers
  - Do you prefer email, text message, or a phone call?
  - What hours are good to call the teacher?
  - How often will you check your emails?
  - Is there a teacher/parent app you use for texting?
- Set up routines for parent volunteers in the classroom
- Determine whether parent–teacher conferences will be in-person, virtual, or both, and communicate how often conferences will occur

Consider the following questions as you reflect on building routines with families.

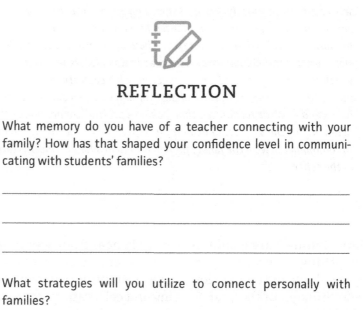

REFLECTION

What memory do you have of a teacher connecting with your family? How has that shaped your confidence level in communicating with students' families?

_____

_____

_____

What strategies will you utilize to connect personally with families?

_____

_____

_____

The Big Ideas

In this chapter, we analyzed how classroom procedures and routines create an efficient and productive environment where all learners are capable of thriving. As you continue synthesizing the habit of procedures and routines, frequently revisit this chapter and observe the effectiveness or challenges of various procedures you and your learners put in place. Consider collaborating with your colleagues or an instructional coach on their best procedures and routines. Lastly, when thinking about setting up your classroom, remember the power of student voice and choice when arranging furniture and developing procedures and routines that create the conditions of success for you and your learners.

Let's Reflect

What resonated with you about the impact of routines on student behavior?

_____

_____

_____

What routines do you want to make sure you have that will support positive and appropriate behavior?

_____

_____

_____

What barriers are you facing that need to be removed for the procedures and routines you want to focus on?

_____

_____

_____

What's Next?

Chapter 6 takes us into the habit of setting goals. We will analyze avenues to create an environment and pathway that will help students collectively set goals while promoting individual motivation. We will identify the need for clear and attainable goals, which allow students to have a vision of where they need to go while providing checkpoints along the way to help them monitor their progress and celebrate their small milestones toward academic growth.

CHAPTER 6

Set Efficient Goals

Lupe Sjuarez, a teacher in Minnesota, started her school year reading, Step Into Student Goal Setting, *by Nordengren (2022). Lupe was passionate about leading her grade-level team and committed to building the habit of goal setting for all students. However, Lupe was rumbling with how to create an environment and pathway that helped her students collectively set goals and build agency while motivating each student.*

Based on beginning-of-the-year assessments, Lupe knew that teaching the grade-level standards would be challenging and recognized the effort that she needed to put into providing scaffolds, differentiation, and enrichment for the various instructional areas and variety of learners she had in her classroom.

While in a team meeting, Lupe was ruminating on the following quote from Nordengren's goal-setting book: "Goals represent the path from beginner to expert. But students do not all take the same path and even are not all headed toward the same destination" (p. 27). During planning time, Lupe shared the quote with her grade-level team and asked them what experience they had with personalized learning and goal setting. It was evident that Lupe had stumbled into an area that the entire team was curious about, and they decided to collectively dive deeper into student goal setting. Lupe and her team talked about various professional and personal goal settings they had made in their lives and the impact those goals had on their own growth and achievements. For example, one teacher on the team had recently lost over 50 pounds. She shared that she had hired a life coach to help her address several habits in her life that she knew needed to change. They decided to first focus on her diet. After accomplishing and celebrating the weight loss milestone, the teacher set a new goal around exercise. As she shared more about her goals and steps that led her to healthier habits, the team continued to think about how personalized goal setting might positively impact student growth and achievement.

WHY GOAL SETTING MATTERS

Extensive research from J. Hattie (2021a) and Marzano (2009) has identified that goal setting has a positive outcome on student growth and achievement. This is largely because goal setting focuses students on specific outcomes and clarifies the relationship between those outcomes and success in the future (Stronge & Grant, 2014). Clear and attainable goals allow students to have a vision of where they need to go while providing checkpoints along the way to help them monitor their progress and celebrate their small milestones toward academic growth. Furthermore, effective goal setting helps students gain clarity around what they are supposed to focus on and purposeful practice that impacts their individual achievements.

> The heart of an effective goal-setting process lies in the students themselves. Whether we choose to acknowledge it or not, students are responsible for when, where, and how they will learn. While a teacher can never force students to apply themselves to the task of learning, there are many tools at the teacher's disposal to motivate and engage students in the hard work of learning. (Nordengren, 2022).

WHAT GOAL SETTING IS . . .	WHAT GOAL SETTING IS NOT . . .
• An ongoing process • Individual to each student • Based on truly inspiring students to master content, not (just) to perform well • A balancing act between what is meaningful with what is attainable	• Something that happens only after a test • Telling students what their goals will be • A way of comparing students to one another • Something done once and never revisited or revised

THE IMPACT OF CLASSROOM GOALS

Setting classroom goals for behavior and academic growth is a powerful habit that yields high achievement. As Nordengren (2022) points out, setting classroom goals has a significant role in laying the groundwork for setting, monitoring and celebrating goals. In addition, classroom goals can help motivate students through supporting their team (class or small group of classmates) as they meet a collective goal, such as putting materials away in a timely manner or building their collective reading stamina by gradually increasing the amount of time spent on independent reading.

Explaining the *why* for the goal and how it will be celebrated or acknowledged is great modeling for the goal-setting process. This type of goal setting helps the class identify an area of growth that is important and allows for students to support and celebrate their collective teamwork. Research around goal setting reminds us to make sure the goals we set are attainable and that it is an ongoing process (Nordengren, 2022). Having students brainstorm ways to meet the collective goal is also an effective way to plan for the conditions of success when using classroom goals.

COLLECTIVE STUDENT EFFICACY AND CLASSROOM CULTURE

> Collective student efficacy is a student's belief that by working with others they will learn more and can be a powerful accelerator of student learning and a precursor to future employment. Furthermore, collective student efficacy is more than cooperative and collaborative learning. Collective efficacy requires the refinement of both individual and collective tasks that build on each other over time. (Hattie et al., 2021)

Hence, setting collective classroom goals also supports teachers in focusing on small, powerful wins when they are managing a diverse group of learners. Often, we see all the negative actions or challenges in our classrooms. But when teachers and students purposely focus on a specific goal, it can shift the mindset and energy in a classroom.

For example, attendance may be a class goal at the secondary level. The teacher may decide to set the attendance goal in a manner that creates positive peer pressure and healthy competition within the classroom. It is important to celebrate the collective group of students every time the class makes progress toward the goal, which helps to create conditions of success for all students.

At the elementary level, a common challenge is that students take too long to gather needed task materials. In this case, the teacher may want to use gathering (pacing) as a class goal. The teacher and class work together to improve the amount of time students spend gathering materials. The team may decide to

Digital goal-setting apps and websites have become extremely popular. While many teachers use these applications to support individual behavior goals, they can also be used to reinforce teamwork and class goals, which often yields positive behavior results and a more positive classroom culture.

use a timer to help make the pacing goal more playful. Once the students collectively start making progress toward the goal, it is essential to celebrate the small milestones.

Use the chart that follows to identify areas that might need classroom behavioral goals in your classroom.

REFLECTION

Identify a challenge that might be impacting your classroom culture.

_____

_____

_____

How could you turn this challenge into a goal?

_____

_____

_____

How long do you anticipate needing this goal? How will you celebrate with your students when you all meet the goal?

_____

_____

_____

How will students be involved in setting and tracking the progress of the goal?

_____

_____

_____

COLLECTIVE ACADEMIC
GROWTH AND ACHIEVEMENT

> The process of setting goals, whether it ends in
> success or failure, teaches students how learning
> works. By interacting with their goals, students learn
> that effort is rewarded, that learning happens over
> time, and that the best response to falling off the
> path is to get back up again . . . But with deliberate
> cultivation, teachers can use goal setting to create a
> context—a culture—in which students learn how to
> learn. (Nordengren, 2022)

Classroom academic goals are similar in nature to collective
classroom culture goals; however, academic goals should
directly tie to content or academic instructional areas. When
a class is working on a collective academic goal, they may
collectively make progress some days and need a restart another
day. Helping students collectively or independently reset when
they fall apart is an incredible opportunity to teach grit and
provides a chance for students to recognize that reaching goals
and learning happen over time.

For example, a language arts goal might be focused on the
habits of reading and writing, where students are directly
working on building their reading or writing stamina. This
habit will clearly impact students' ability to focus on reading
or writing and purposefully practice partner or independent
reading or writing, which will have a direct impact on growth
and achievement in language arts. The teacher may create a
goal for stamina for the day and/or week after modeling what
the habit of reading or writing stamina should and should not
look like and even use a timer to help kids monitor their reading
focus or stamina over a week or month. In addition, the teacher
may ask for a certain amount of writing to be done in a set
amount of time. Sometimes grade levels may have classroom
competitions for their collective stamina. Creating a stamina
competition within small groups in the class or with other
classes can create an added element of novelty. At the end of
the week, the class or small group of students that has had the
longest amount of time actively engaging in reading or writing
may be celebrated.

Reflect with your team on opportunities that goal setting for the
collective group could impact growth.

REFLECTION

What academic themes or trends do you think all students could use support with (e.g., math fact fluency, reading stamina, habits when they get stuck or do not understand a task)?

_____

_____

_____

How will you share this trend with your students and set a classroom goal?

_____

_____

_____

How will you track progress and provide feedback with the goal?

_____

_____

_____

How will you celebrate the goal? Is the goal broken down small enough so you can celebrate small milestones with the group?

_____

_____

_____

GOAL SETTING AND PERSONALIZED LEARNING PLANS FOR INDIVIDUAL STUDENTS

Most instructional time spent in classrooms focuses on the collective group or a standards-based learning task. However, it is important for students to have individual academic and behavioral goals. When teachers set up systems that target personalized learning goals for students, this positively impacts the teacher–student relationship and academic growth and achievement of each learner. Students should receive support with their personalized learning goals through small groups or one-on-one mini sessions to help each student meet their own academic or behavioral goals. Creating systems or "habits" in the classroom to both set and monitor goals can be done *with* students instead of *for* students. When students can participate in the decision-making of their learning goals, they tend to buy into the learning process and are more willing to work through the challenges of their learning goals. In his work, Nordengren (2022) echoes the positive impact on behavioral growth and academic achievement that one-on-one conversations between teachers and students can have on goal setting habits.

Creating systems or "habits" in the classroom to both set and monitor goals can be done with *students instead of* for *students.*

When students have behavioral goals, it is important to consider their privacy and emotional wellbeing when setting, reflecting, and celebrating their personal goals. For example, a student who has a tough time focusing and consistently has their phone out may need a goal to limit time with or access to their technology during specific instructional times each day. This type of goal may create healthier habits while honoring the students' desire to connect with the world on their phones. Another example of a behavioral goal might be focused on blurting out in class during direct or whole group instruction. To help the student gather data related to the goal, you might have them work on tallying how frequently they blurt out during a certain amount of time. Conferencing with the student to reflect on the "blurting data" they recorded will help determine next steps. If the student blurted out six times in an hour, the goal for the rest of the week may be cutting the blurting to four times.

When setting behavioral goals, it is important that students do not feel ashamed of the behaviors but that they see the goals as a way to improve themselves. When students understand how a specific behavior might limit their full potential and have voice and choice, the behavioral goal is more likely to improve. However, like all goals, it is important for the teacher to help set attainable goals in collaboration with the student that can be monitored frequently and celebrated along the way. Behavioral goals should be achieved respectfully and remain between the student and teacher. If a teacher corrects a student in front of their peers or celebrates the student with a behavioral goal, it can humiliate or feel like shame for the student. It is important to be mindful of respecting the individual student's emotional needs and privacy when considering behavioral goals.

Setting academic personalized learning goals is like the process of setting behavioral goals. Inviting students to analyze data with you to determine a personalized learning goal helps students to feel valued, builds their self-efficacy, and encourages them to own their own learning. For example, sharing adaptive assessment data that helps students to identify instructional areas of strength and areas for growth can help students to recognize an area to celebrate and an area to hone in on. Once the goal is set, the teacher and student monitor progress frequently using data and regular conferencing/one-on-one discussions and adjust the goal as needed as the student makes progress. It is important to celebrate success as students make progress toward their goal in order to encourage them and build their self-efficacy.

Use the questions that follow to reflect on how to use data to determine personalized learning goals with students.

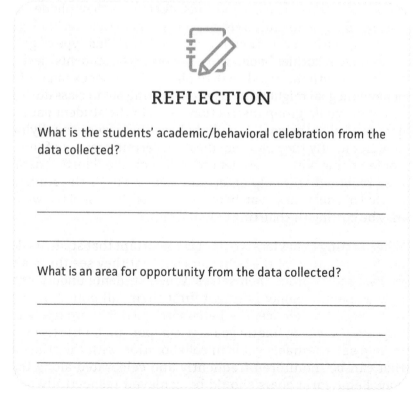

REFLECTION

What is the students' academic/behavioral celebration from the data collected?

_____

_____

_____

What is an area for opportunity from the data collected?

_____

_____

_____

What does the student believe about the data? What do they think they need to work on?

_____

_____

_____

What barriers does the student think may impact this goal?

_____

_____

_____

How much time is needed to complete the goal? Will they need the goal to be progress monitored?

_____

_____

_____

USING GOAL NOTEBOOKS TO SUPPORT PERSONALIZED LEARNING GOALS

Teachers and students benefit from systems, materials, and structures that help them develop, practice, track, reflect on, and assess their personalized learning goals. Creating a goal notebook or folder they bring to their one-on-one conferences will let the student and teacher reflect on the progress and support needed within the personalized learning goal. For example, if a student is working on reading and writing inflected endings, the teacher may create a T-chart in the student's goal notebook that allows the student to both remember and build on their learning. The purpose of this notebook is not to fill it with cute worksheets that support the learning goal but rather create an authentic, explicit support that helps the student focus and practice the learning intention.

Primary Grade Example

Goal: Read and write words with -*ed* endings. Find words as you read and write that have the -*ed* inflected ending. Sort the words in the -*ed* chart that follows.

WORDS THAT END WITH THE -ed SOUND	WORDS THAT END WITH THE d SOUND	WORDS THAT END WITH THE t SOUND
grounded	used	walked
excited	loved	danced

Secondary Grade Example

Goal: Use context clues to identify unknown words in the book you are currently reading independently.

UNKNOWN WORD	PAGE YOU FOUND IT ON	TYPE OF CONTEXT CLUE YOU USED	WHAT YOU THINK IT MIGHT MEAN
plant	32	description	factory

Once the student has found unfamiliar words and is ready to share their learning goal with you, the teacher and student use the goal notebook or folder to revisit it. Keeping track of students' learning goals can be overwhelming for teachers, and this allows students to take ownership of their own learning while holding them accountable for progressing on the goal. The goal notebook or folder can then travel home so that parents also are aware of the students' progress on their learning goals.

Providing time for students to work on their personal learning goal is essential. A simple procedure or routine to support this habit is having students pull out their goal folders after independently reading and working for five to ten minutes on their goals. This allows the teacher to carefully monitor the students working on their goals. While watching students work, the teacher can determine if students have misconceptions or are mastering their goals. This intentional student observation allows the teacher to purposefully create a new one-on-one conference schedule. Students with misconceptions may need an urgent appointment/conference with you while others are still progressing through their goal. Other learners may need more time prior to meeting with you to work independently. The routine of a goal notebook that students use frequently will help them and the teacher remain organized while monitoring progress toward the individual goal.

Reflect on the following questions around procedures and routines with monitoring and setting goals.

REFLECTION

What are your current challenges with tracking individualized learning goals?

_____

_____

_____

What resources do you want/need when setting and monitoring goals with your students?

_____

_____

_____

What are your next steps with setting up procedures and routines for individualized learning goals?

_____

_____

_____

PROVIDING FEEDBACK WHILE ASSESSING AND ANALYZING GOALS

It is important to provide feedback to your class and individual students as they make progress toward their learning/behavioral goals. It is especially effective to provide specific feedback around a task and invite students into analyzing the task as well. For example, if a class goal is to increase the overall reading stamina of the group, it is important to have students reflect collectively on their progress in addition to receiving feedback from you as the teacher. Stopping every day after independent reading and checking in with students on the goal allows for learners to evaluate their collective progress. When we quickly breeze over the stamina goal and say, "good job" or "well done," this does not allow students to self-correct or celebrate the small milestones of their progress. Feedback that is more specific to the task helps students to understand and reflect more strategically on the goal. For example, saying, "I noticed that everyone's eyes were focused on their books and not looking around the room today," provides clear feedback of the stamina goal and careful monitoring so that the students can collectively celebrate the small milestone.

When working with individual students during their one-on-one mini goal setting conferences, it is essential to provide feedback on the progression of learning within the personalized learning goal. For example, if a student is working on using context clues from the text to support their vocabulary development, the teacher and student can look up the words that the student documented in their goal notebook and determine if/which context clues they are using. The teacher can help the student to analyze their work and provide specific feedback on their goal. Again, this feedback should be noticeably clear and more detailed than, "You did a great job." Providing clear feedback around vocabulary may sound like, "You are using the description and definition context clues effectively. Next, we will need to work on using inferences to determine unknown words." Providing specific feedback to a student on their goal is invaluable.

The Big Ideas

In this chapter, you focused on the impact of how to set, monitor, and organize classroom goals and personalized learning goals for your students. Explicit tasks or activities should be adjusted frequently for learners as they move through their learning goals. In addition, these individualized learning goals should be based on what the student is ready to learn next. Feedback and frequent goal setting during one-on-one conferring with students will keep their individualized learning goals front and center. Additionally, establishing clear procedures and routines—such as a goal setting notebook or folder—can also help students and teachers promote a meaningful process that promotes and impacts the student's academic growth and achievement path.

Let's Reflect

How have you personally used goal setting in your own life?

_____

_____

_____

_____

What goals have you set with your grade-level or content-area team? How did that impact team dynamics? How did that impact student growth?

_____

_____

_____

_____

What type of class goals have you set with your students? How has this impacted classroom culture?

_____

_____

_____

_____

What type of goal setting have you done with individual students? How has that impacted their growth and achievement? How has goal setting impacted students' self-efficacy?

_____

_____

_____

_____

What's Next?

In Chapter 7, we will continue our journey with the powerful habit of feedback. While each habit in this book has qualities of its own, many of the habits are woven together. You will see the direct connection between goal setting and effective feedback in Chapter 7. Chapter 7 also discusses the importance of proactively seeking feedback so you can continuously grow and improve as an educator. By understanding the key characteristics of effective feedback, you will learn how to identify individuals who can provide you that useful, targeted feedback and develop specific processes for asking them for support.

Get and Use Feedback Effectively

Tamara was navigating her fourth year of teaching freshman English language arts (ELA) when she began to explore the use of Socratic Seminars to engage her students more deeply in their discussions of To Kill a Mockingbird. *She was excited to also build students' speaking and listening skills. Because it was her first year implementing the strategy in person (post-pandemic learning), she faced some hurdles in guiding students to function independently and move into more critical thinking and analysis. Her friend, a fellow ELA teacher with several years of experience, heard her concerns and offered to come watch a lesson to offer feedback. Tamara was thrilled. Reading the email that ensued following the visit, however, she was left feeling a bit perplexed. Her colleague's comments were entirely positive—not a bad thing—but gave her no information on where to improve. Something about this experience just did not meet Tamara's hopes, but why?*

THE IMPORTANCE OF FEEDBACK

When was the last time you participated in the exercise of being observed by a supervisor while teaching—perhaps your principal or another leader in the school? In most common scenarios, the observer shared some form of information back with you. Perhaps they reported facts, or maybe they offered reflective questions and followed up with a discussion. While the observer may believe that the focus of the observation is to cultivate your growth as a professional, the feedback provided may not always yield that result. Did you see their feedback as connected to your practice? Perhaps the outcome offered little meaning or context, giving you the feeling that getting feedback is a negative experience. Sound familiar? To engage in micro-shifts of practice for your continued development, consider actively seeking the information you need!

Feedback is input from external sources on any particular practice or skill that you aim to develop or grow. Receiving feedback, when rooted and framed in a learner-empowered mindset, is not only highly impactful but is also entirely within your realm of control as to how, when, and why to receive that feedback. As teachers, that impact on expertise helps you to achieve your ultimate goal: high levels of learning for all kids. Participating in teacher coaching—where teachers receive direct and instant feedback on their instruction—shows sizable impacts on outcomes for students of coached teachers (Kraft et al., 2017). Specific, corrective, and/or positive feedback improves practice for teachers newly entering the profession (Scheeler et al., 2004) and for veterans (Garet et al., 2017). Of course, your supervisor will always decide when to conduct an evaluative observation, but there is power in getting feedback in many other ways! Feedback can be a purpose-driven, empowering experience that helps you to grow as a proactive problem-solver, a collaborative thought-partner, and a highly effective teacher.

EFFECTIVE FEEDBACK IS . . .	EFFECTIVE FEEDBACK IS NOT . . .
• Clear and specific	• Vague advice or general praise (e.g., "Good job!")
• Actionable and inspires change	• Demotivating
• Targeted toward a goal or next step	• Unrelated to a clear purpose
• Asset-based, building upon strengths	• Highlighting of weakness or deficiencies, deficit based
• Constructive	• Evaluative
• Rooted in a learner-empowered purpose	• Rooted in a learner "manager" purpose

USING FEEDBACK AS A STEPPING STONE

The practices of giving and receiving feedback are more than just valuable in themselves. Danielson (2013) describes how feedback is integral to a number of other skills and opportunities and can be a stepping stone to enhance your work in the teaching profession. Teachers who regularly practice giving feedback are better suited to take on classroom research, support student teachers, facilitate student groups, and engage in other work that lets them expand their influence beyond their own classroom. Receiving feedback well can enable teachers to engage with new resources—like instructional coaches—which has proven to deepen the impact of their practice on student outcomes (Hattie, 2021a; Wisniewski et al., 2020). No matter what systems of feedback are in place in your school or district, practicing the skills of feedback can give you the ability to tap into a variety of other tools to enhance your practice.

WHY WE MIGHT AVOID FEEDBACK

Your current comfort level with giving and especially receiving feedback is likely based on past experiences. Maybe you have had great experiences and welcome any and all feedback. But perhaps you have experienced feedback negatively, which has led to feelings of uncertainty or apprehension around the process. Perhaps you have experienced one of these scenarios:

- As a teacher, you operate in an environment where, no matter your years of experience, you are expected to be the expert in the room. But when performance evaluations were administered, you weren't treated as an "expert in the room," and the process felt very unsupportive.

- In your teacher preparation program, you learned a bevy of information about effective practices. But at your first teaching job, the teachers around you may implement those practices inconsistently or not at all (Scheeler et al., 2004), leaving you confused.

- You work in a school where student achievement results are below average, and it feels as though evaluators make negative assumptions about your teaching practice, leading you to find feedback uncomfortable.

Based on experiences like these or others, you may want to avoid proactively seeking feedback. Yet seeking and acting upon feedback can develop a growth-oriented mindset, foster collaboration, and lead to improved teaching skills. Further, teaching demands that we frequently try new approaches and embrace the need for adaptation to ensure we meet the needs of all learners. With the practices in this chapter, you'll be empowered to adopt the curiosity-rich mindset of an avid learner who sees the continuous process of growth as an enjoyable journey!

HOW TO DEVELOP THE HABIT
OF ASKING FOR FEEDBACK

Developing the skill of seeking and utilizing feedback is an effective response to the demands of an uncertain teaching environment in which success is predicated on your ability to adapt. When you proactively approach the feedback experience with a purpose, engage intentionally with others, and apply the feedback to your work, you'll gain confidence in your ability to navigate each day as its own exciting learning opportunity.

BEGIN WITH PURPOSE

Before you embark on a quest for gathering feedback to improve, first consider the different forms feedback may take and their purpose. Feedback can often be mistaken for validation, particularly in the case where the relationship between the giver and receiver is not clearly safe and free from supervisory implications. Feedback may also feel transactional, as if you must provide some form of commentary back to a colleague if they comment on your well-designed lesson plan, whether you have anything authentic to say or not. Before seeking feedback, first identify what it is that you hope to gain. Do you simply need to know if you are achieving expectations? Perhaps you would benefit from input on your progress toward a goal you are working on after reading Chapter 6, or perhaps you are curious about how to improve a process, a project, or even a relationship. Clearly defining *what* you need from the feedback you are seeking will ensure it is utmost meaningful and impactful.

WHOM TO ASK AND WHEN

When you seek feedback for the purpose of continuous improvement, you will likely recognize the myriad possibilities all around you to engage and grow. A school is a rich environment filled with countless experts who have unique insights and skills. What might be the purpose of seeking feedback from these various individuals or groups?

Supervisors: Despite the assumption that supervisors may only give you feedback that is corrective, school leaders inherently want all teachers to succeed, just as they do their students. In fact, they rely on the success of teachers more than perhaps any other factor to ensure the school achieves its purpose. It's understandable if, even knowing this, you become anxious at the prospect of being observed, and your stomach turns knots when the resulting observation notes are delivered. Shifting your mindset toward ownership of your professional growth places you in the driver's seat, however. Your interest in pushing your limits or calibrating the effectiveness of your teaching practices will also let your boss know you are passionate about improvement! When asking an administrator for feedback, consider the following key strategies:

1. **Areas of expertise:** Is your supervisor a former math teacher? Do they lead professional development on social-emotional learning in your school? Knowing your supervisor's strengths will help you match your needs to what they can offer.

2. **Your goals:** Before you even ask, be crystal clear about where you want to grow. Did you gather some data revealing a need to improve your transitions in class? Perhaps the procedures you've implemented on transitions aren't impacting student engagement the way you hoped? Prepare to identify exactly what you want your supervisor to look for.

3. **Time:** Everyone in schools is typically incredibly busy, including you. When seeking feedback from your supervisor, approach the request with a time frame for the visit and exactly when you can meet to debrief or if an email will suffice.

4. **Don't take it personally:** Be prepared that your supervisor may say no or that the experience may not be as meaningful as you hoped. Don't stress! In the complex work of school leadership, your supervisor may not be able to control what consumes their time.

5. **Show gratitude:** Above all else, thank your supervisor for their time and contributions to your growth.

Mentors or instructional coaches: On the off chance you are fortunate to teach in a school where mentors are paired with teachers or where there are instructional coaches on staff, you've hit the jackpot! These roles are designed to support the growth and improvement of teachers. Consider asking your supervisor to set you up with a mentor, if you don't already have one, or if mentors aren't available, seek someone who does not work in your school but who demonstrates a willingness to support you. Instructional coaches or any other type of coach in your school or district may be assigned to specifically conduct observations on a schedule. But remember, you are in charge here—create an experience for collecting their feedback on any specific skill you are learning or exploring. As an example, perhaps you have received feedback from a supervisor but feel reluctant to get their continued input on your progress. Consider requesting a coaching cycle experience instead. In a coaching cycle, you share the feedback with your instructional coach, identify what you plan to implement in an upcoming class where they can come and observe, and meet to reflect on success immediately after. A mentor, on the other hand, can support you in other ways. They are a great source of support for debriefing on what you learned in the coaching cycle, or they could also invite you to observe them in action and compare your practice against that of a model. All of these are rich opportunities to grow!

Critical friends: Critical friends are not just any friends. According to the National School Reform Faculty (2022), Critical Friends Group© (CFG) communities consist of five to twelve members who commit to improving their practice through collaborative learning and structured interactions (protocols) and meet at least once a month for about two hours. In fact, the National School Reform Faculty (2022) describes Critical Friends Groups (CFG®) as a structured protocol not unlike professional learning communities (PLCs).

The Critical Friends Group protocol offers a structured process for an in-depth analysis of an essential question in a group setting. For example, a teacher may be grappling with the question, "Why can't my students accomplish this work?" or "Why is there so much peer-to-peer conflict among my students?" Led by a neutral facilitator, participants rotate through a cycle of questions and discussion with specific goals: surfacing meaning and external reality, then eliciting resolution and identifying next steps. The result can be a deep, rich understanding of a complex issue faced by an individual or a group, with a collaborative, solution-focused orientation.

Whether using the CFG protocol or not, an experience of learning with and from Critical Friends can entail classroom observations with debriefing, analysis of student work samples, or an investigation into student learning outcomes to determine next steps, among other activities. The nature of this experience should entail a mutual exchange of feedback and center around a specific focus of practice, thus requiring intentional planning as a pair or a group who wishes to grow together. There is no limit, however, to the duration and frequency of interactions you wish to design because, remember, you're in charge of this journey! Taking time to learn and practice the skills involved in thoughtful examination of practice, providing and receiving targeted feedback, and intentionally applying the learning will yield the most impactful results for this type of work.

Colleagues: Across the campus, down the hall, or at the lunch table, you may find countless venues for interacting informally with colleagues who teach the same grade level or subject as you, making them a great choice for a source of feedback as you strive to grow. Remember, however, that validation is not the intent here. It can be intimidating for a peer to critique your work, not to mention awkward to receive such information if proper groundwork is not laid. Colleagues are a great resource for very targeted feedback using specific questions that are aligned with an area of their own expertise. Maybe you are aware of a peer who excels at formative assessment, for instance, and you aim to improve—here's a perfect opportunity to team up and learn from them. Start with a focus that is narrow or small—verifying that your lesson plans include appropriate scaffolding steps, for example. Advise your colleague that you're trying to improve and want their candid opinion, not just approval, and be sure to thank them for helping you get better!

When André first started teaching sixth-grade math, he was disappointed in the amount of growth his students accomplished on benchmark assessments in the first half of the year. Struggling to understand potential sources of the lack of growth, he couldn't help but make assumptions about the impact of student absences and the overall interrupted learning experiences of the COVID-19 pandemic in prior years. Reading about microteaching in PLC+ (Fisher & Frey, 2019), he sought out his classroom neighbor to gather some feedback, entailing a review of brief video clips of himself teaching. André specifically asked his colleague to determine if his students appeared to be engaging with his instruction at the level he was aiming for. Through this constructive feedback protocol, André learned he was unaware of some missing academic vocabulary the students needed to solve the problems. He chose to gather some formative student data to identify with more clarity, then respond with targeted instruction to support his students. By adopting a learner's mindset toward solving a problem of practice, André gained valuable feedback, which guided his next efforts, and both he and his students grew as a result.

Students' guardians: The COVID-19 pandemic deeply impacted our schools and our personal lives in devastating ways. But reflecting on the sudden immersion teachers experienced into their students' lives, there may be a silver lining: Educators recognized the inextricable connection between the school and the home. Guardians may or may not be highly engaged in their child's schooling, but your most thoroughly planned efforts at bringing in their support can also miss the mark. Seeking feedback from them can offer powerful insights into relationship-building strategies that unite you with families in support of your students' learning. Seem risky? Taking proactive steps to request guardians' opinions and feedback on specific areas may actually serve to mitigate conflict-oriented environments. People value being asked for advice—whether on the clarity of the information found in the weekly newsletter, the strategies they find effective for calming their child when upset, or a myriad of other topics. Bringing them into your improvement journey is likely to reap rewards, including strengthened school–guardian relationships, a known factor in improving student learning outcomes (Hart et al., 2020).

Tips for asking guardians for feedback:

- **Focus questions on things that you can control.** Examples include communication methods, scheduling of volunteers, or their child's favorite school experiences. Don't place yourself in a difficult situation by asking for ideas on instructional resources that you likely won't be able to (or want to) adjust!

- **Respect their time.** Consider gathering multiple topics over time and grouping them into one survey rather than weekly questions.

- **Be prepared to share general themes from the feedback.** Convey the feedback as a meaningful, improvement-oriented process for both parties.

- **Encourage participation and minimize concerns by making self-identification optional.** If you ask guardians to provide feedback on your communication practices (frequency, topics, etc.), end with the statement, "Would you be open to discussing this further, if needed? If so, please share your name and email here."

Students: The most important purpose of all your work is student learning, so why not gather feedback from the students themselves? Now, asking students if you differentiate effectively is not the goal here—they aren't trained professionals, after all. However, the decisions you make about your classroom may or may not always have the impact you intend, and students of every age are a wonderful source for telling you about their "classroom experience." Students can be invited to share feedback in individual conversations, for starters; consider asking them whether a recent assessment provided them the opportunity to fully show what they understand about a concept. Offering a survey to the class can provide a lens on classroom culture—from students' confidence level in collaborative work to their feeling psychologically safe, to whether the learning experiences are too hard, too easy, or just right. One of the most powerful results of inviting student feedback is students who are empowered and thus more likely to engage in the learning.

Ben, a fifth-grade teacher, noticed that not all his students seemed willing to speak up in class. Was it shyness? Uncertainty about the content? Did they feel they could not be themselves and speak freely in front of others? He hoped to develop a classroom culture with high levels of discourse, so he created a survey for his students and conveyed to them why he was collecting their input. He kept his questions brief and offered a combination of multiple-choice scales and open responses for a chance to gain specific details in their answers. With the responses he received, Ben identified a few key areas for adapting his classroom culture. He shared these specific actions with the students and let them know that the changes were derived from their survey responses. For example, he created a procedure and trained students to use a bank of ideas so they could build confidence in asking thoughtful questions. He also changed several grouping arrangements to support a more comfortable dynamic among individuals. Later, he repeated an abbreviated version of the survey to measure the effect of his changes, thereby modeling the iterative opportunities presented when feedback is viewed as a purposeful process meant to guide new efforts after making changes. He celebrated the results of the modifications with the class as they grew in their abilities to build on one another's ideas and respond thoughtfully to diverse perspectives.

Professional learning networks: Have you ever attended a conference and returned to school energized and excited to test-drive your new learning? Then, perhaps faced with teammates who didn't join you or weren't sure what the buzz was about, your enthusiasm fizzled and you drifted back to the original routine? Professional learning networks (Rincon-Gallardo & Fullan, 2016) are a powerful antidote to the siloed structure of working in one school, and the internet is the playground! Networking with fellow educators can happen on a Twitter chat, in a Zoom meeting, at a conference, or even via text. Among a group of fellow educators in the field, feedback opportunities abound. Beware of the distinction between constructive feedback and validation when pursuing these opportunities; rather, develop focused and intentional requests just as you would for a principal or a coach. For example, maybe you attended a workshop on design-thinking, and the strategies fell a little flat in your classroom. Frame two to three specific questions about your problem and reach out to the trainer who gave the workshop—you might be surprised how quickly and effectively they answer you!

WHOM TO ASK	AREAS OF PRACTICE WHERE THEY MIGHT OFFER USEFUL FEEDBACK
Supervisors	Classroom instruction Leadership development Collaboration skills
Mentors or instructional coaches	Skill development, such as lesson planning, assessment design, etc. Specific teaching skills focused on a growth goal, such as increasing engagement, improving classroom management, etc.
Critical friends	Help examining student work samples against lesson plans to identify causes of results Help reviewing student behavior data before and after implementing an intervention
Colleagues	Observation of instruction when implementing a new strategy or practice Review of communication (to guardians, students, or even supervisors)
Students' guardians	Communication efforts Support provided to their child Strategies to engage their child
Students	Classroom culture Impact of instruction Perceptions of teacher's efforts, such as support, etc.
Professional learning network	Instructional practices, such as differentiation, assessment, etc. Expertise on implementing new strategies or instructional practices, such as project-based learning

WHAT YOU ASK MATTERS

By now, you may have developed your list of those you would invite to join you on your professional growth journey, and the time has come to determine what you will ask them and how. The ability to maximize the value of feedback relies on being intentional in your questions and engagement with others as much as it does on putting the feedback into use. Consider the difference between these two questions, and imagine the potential response to each:

1. How did I do?

   OR

2. I am trying to get better at increasing the depth of knowledge-level of questions I ask students. How can I improve, based on what you observed?

Effective questions are essential to maximize the time and expertise of your feedback source, as well as to get the most actionable information for yourself. Specificity is key. Focus the question on a skill, strategy, or behavior. If relevant, reference the event during which you were observed demonstrating said skill. Then, get to the point! "How could I improve?" or "What is one thing I could do more of?" Or even perhaps, "If I were to do one thing differently next time, what would you suggest?" With practice, you will become an expert at formulating questions that generate highly useful feedback!

Read the example that follows. Then use this tool to help you generate effective questions when seeking feedback from others.

Example: Rebecca hopes to develop better success criteria in her lesson plans. Rebecca's mentor, an experienced teacher, led staff professional learning on building success criteria.

IDENTIFY WHAT YOU AIM TO IMPROVE OR WHERE YOU HOPE TO GROW	CONNECT THE FEEDBACK PROVIDER'S EXPERTISE TO YOUR GROWTH AREA	ADD AN OPEN-ENDED QUESTION
I am working on improving the connection between my success criteria and the standard I'm teaching.	I remember the training you led us through, and I thought your examples were exactly what I hope to create for my plans.	Can you tell me what strengths and growth areas you see in these plans for my next unit?

As guardian–teacher conferences approach, Rachel wants to incorporate new ways in which she will communicate with families about their child's learning progression. Simply sharing the current percentage and the list of assignments they have not completed or the cursory, "Everything's great! Keep up the good work!" commentary will not suffice. Prior to conferences, she sets up a visit with her department chair to share the list of key points she has developed and gathers feedback on two primary questions:

1. *Is my word-choice appropriate in the statements?*

2. *Am I missing any key information that will help the guardian understand the report card?*

She also invites her department chair to join her first conference and listen in, specifically focusing on whether Rachel fully answers any questions the guardian brings forward. Rachel and her department chair debriefed shortly after the conference on this focus point. The keys to her success?

- *Clear understanding of what information she wanted*

- *A reasonable number of targeted questions to ask her colleague*

- *Highly specific communication with the department chair*

- *Follow-through on application of the feedback with an observation*

When Rachel first approached the department chair, she didn't begin with a plea for help; nor did she pose her request in a general frame—such as "How does this look?" Rather, she explicitly started the discussion with, "I'm working on making sure that guardians understand the information in the new report cards, and I'd appreciate your feedback on what I have developed. I have a few specific questions and would value your expertise." By Rachel's placing the notion of seeking feedback squarely in the realm of professional input, the interaction is no longer at risk of seeming like a judgment or damaging to their relationship.

RESOURCES FOR PUTTING FEEDBACK TO WORK

When feedback is provided, no amount of detail and specificity can compel you to embrace it as an impetus for change unless you believe in the need to adjust your behavior, attitude, or practice. When you proactively seek the input that could help you grow and improve, you are already one step closer to achieving that growth. That said, don't let it go to waste!

Use the template that follows to practice purposefully gathering feedback before beginning the next section on applying feedback.

REFLECTION

Identify a specific growth area of your teaching practice (questioning strategies, formative assessment design, guardian communication, etc.): _____

Whom will you ask? What is their role? Why are they the best choice?

_____

_____

_____

On what specific area of this teaching skill/practice would you like them to offer feedback?

_____

_____

_____

When can you set up the opportunity for them to observe or review the focus area?

_____

_____

_____

What will you do with the feedback? (e.g., compare it to your own self-reflection, integrate it into other feedback sources to identify themes, or apply it to a new setting in your work)

_____

_____

_____

Curious about even more ways to collect feedback and personal growth ideas? Consider these ideas:

- Complete a Clifton Strengths Finder assessment (https://www.gallup.com/cliftonstrengths/) and analyze your results in comparison to other feedback you've received.

- Connect your feedback to your long-term goals or a personal development plan.

- Identify a role model in your field and ask them what skills they feel are crucial to their success.

- Bring your feedback analysis to your next evaluation meeting with your supervisor and share with them areas where you are working toward growth.

STEPS FOR APPLYING NEW FEEDBACK

1. **Review the information, compare responses, and look for themes.** It is important to identify the elements that are actionable (and be sure to appreciate those affirmations of your hard work, too!) and create a space to save them—digital or otherwise.

2. **Ask yourself clarifying questions.** By asking yourself these questions, you are seeking to relate the information to yourself or your teaching practices. This will enable you to make generalizations that you can act upon. Some example questions include the following: How does this information connect to your work as a teacher? Are they new ideas you had not thought of? Or, perhaps, are they aligned with your hunches about improvement areas that you had not yet acted upon?

3. **Organize priorities and integrate next steps into your daily calendar.** Resist the urge to tackle every item you've identified. Think quality over quantity: Two points or twelve, it does not matter—the list may evolve over time. It is also important to sort the items according to a timeline. Ask yourself, What can I reasonably apply immediately? Which ones will take more time? Are there others that require further learning first?

In the next chapter, Prioritizing Amidst a Sea of Initiatives, you'll gain some key strategies for mastering these skills!

The Big Ideas

In this chapter, you explored the importance of proactively seeking feedback on all areas of your work so you can continuously grow and improve as an educator. By understanding the key characteristics of effective feedback, you can then identify individuals who could provide you that useful, targeted feedback and develop specific processes for asking them for support. As you define the types of questions to ask, for example, or the purpose that feedback from a supervisor can serve as opposed to that of the students in your class, you will build a sophisticated toolbox that you can utilize for the rest of your career! Amid uncertainty and constant change, developing your ability to nimbly adapt, learn, and grow will ensure you thrive no matter the current environment, and feedback is crucial to your success in this area.

Let's Reflect

What new ideas have extended your thoughts on the concept of feedback to support your professional growth and development?

_____

_____

_____

How might the skills you learned in the chapter on procedures and routines aid you in applying your learning from this chapter on feedback?

_____

_____

_____

How do you envision the art of getting and using feedback as supporting your ability to align your work with your purpose identified in Chapter 1?

_____

_____

_____

What's Next?

Chapter 8 takes us on a journey through organizational skills that empower you to control your schedule and accomplish short- and long-term goals. We will explore ways to evolve from always addressing the "urgent" to prioritizing the important and ensuring a consistent focus on the work at hand: ensuring the highest levels of learning by every single one of our students!

Prioritize Amidst a Sea of Initiatives

As Amy, a high school Spanish teacher, sat down during her planning time, she hurriedly sorted through the collection of exit tickets her students had submitted at the end of Spanish II the preceding morning. She was just getting to know her students and needed to understand where there were misconceptions before introducing the next standard. She had every intention of reviewing the exit tickets before class, but a dozen new emails in her inbox had consumed her attention instead. She then adjusted her afternoon schedule to create time between the gym and dinner to look the tickets over, as she knew the information would be crucial for the next class session. But somehow, even that adjusted time she had planned went awry, and she ended up entering a few grades instead. And so she found herself quickly planning last minute— exactly what she had tried NOT to do—frustrated that she might let down her students and her expectations of herself for not prioritizing the exit ticket review. For being only September, this was a pattern that was becoming awfully common, and Amy wondered whether she could improve.

WHY PRIORITIZATION MATTERS

The decisions made by teachers—no matter how small or significant—have tremendous implications for the entire ecosystem of the classroom (Eggleston, 2019; McCarty et al., 2021). Some estimates suggest the quantity of decisions teachers make in a single day may be near 1,500! Teachers are asked to receive large quantities of information from diverse sources on a constant basis, interpret the details with that information, and determine an effective response on a prompt basis for a myriad questions or problems at any given time. Time to analyze and reflect on such decisions is scarce yet crucial in order to act in a manner that achieves a desired result. The impact of intensive levels of information-processing, decision-making, and problem analysis teachers face can lead to increased stress, anxiety, and hopelessness. Worse yet, self-confidence and joy can diminish, impacting your relationships with students and leaving purposeful classroom instruction as a last-minute endeavor.

Developing the habit of prioritization, with practice and persistence, can help calm the deluge of information into a more navigable flow with predictable order and manageable timelines. By improving prioritization skills, you are also likely to experience a secondary positive outcome: increased agency. "Teacher agency has been described as teachers' intentional efforts to act in accordance with their beliefs, goals, and knowledge as they engage with their various working contexts" (Toom et al., 2015). When practicing prioritization, we are exerting control over external factors that influence our life, and by doing so, we offset perceptions that we are powerless in a situation. This enables us to plot a deliberate course toward the future and move intentionally toward any goal that we set. As we embrace this decision-making skill of prioritization, our confidence increases in tandem with our sense of agency, and we are enabled to move in a direction of our choosing that is fulfilling, gratifying, and rewarding.

FIGURE 8.1 ● Prioritization Flow

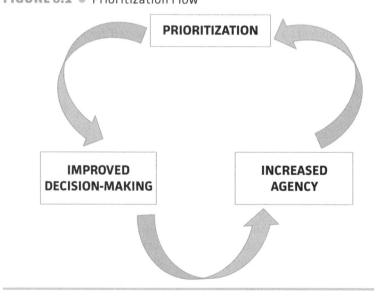

WHAT IT MEANS TO BE A SKILLED PRIORITIZER

Prioritization is in itself a form of decision-making. Given the plethora of decisions a teacher faces each and every day, not all of them require being sorted by priority, however. For example, if we waited to pose probing questions to our students until we collected their first responses, analyzed them, and decided how to proceed, we would miss precious opportunities for on-the-spot formative assessments. Rather, a teacher who is talented at prioritization can efficiently analyze the demands posed by a problem in need of a solution to gauge how those demands will fit into the schema of other existing tasks and plan the "when" and "how" that the response will be executed. When you develop the routine practice of prioritizing, you free up your mental bandwidth to proactively pursue other tasks.

The ego never fails to overestimate what we can accomplish in a day. Knowing this, when you are learning to determine what to prioritize, be conservative and realistic with your expectations. A powerful outcome of prioritization practices is to break down the whole process of achieving a huge task into one that is realistic and manageable with daily, digestible micro-actions.

PRIORITIZATION IS . . .	PRIORITIZATION IS NOT . . .
• A way to control the impact we experience from a constant flow of information and expectations	• Effective when only applied during extremely busy times
• Best practiced in consistent, ongoing intervals	• Impossible! Practiced in small steps at first, it becomes exponentially easier with time
• Essential for sustaining personal wellbeing during disruption and change	• A complete cure for other systemic issues, such as burnout
• Easily integrated into other habits, such as goal setting or procedures and routines	• Limited to making task lists

HOW TO EFFECTIVELY PRIORITIZE TASKS

Developing skills in prioritization begins with understanding the factors that influence your use of time. From there, you can begin to apply responsive action strategies to organize information, filter the urgency of need, and determine when and how you can accomplish required tasks. If we consider the input of information—the "clutter"—a teacher receives in a typical work week, it's easy to recognize that time is one of the most significant challenges faced around effective prioritization. However, there are other obstacles that can hinder our ability to gain confident control of the prioritization process. This section will examine root causes that influence your time and decisions, how to know when you are experiencing the effects of such a root cause, and strategies for overcoming these obstacles.

PROBLEM: TEACHERS FEEL VOICELESS AND OVERWHELMED

ROOT CAUSE: RAPID INSTITUTIONAL CHANGE

Schools are in a constant state of evolution, pursuing changes of varying degrees nearly all of the time. In response to the seismic interruption to "normal" that the world experienced during the COVID-19 pandemic, that evolution may feel as though it is occurring at warp speed. Schools and districts, though well-intended, are tying themselves in knots to accelerate student learning and eliminate opportunity gaps, but all the changes have a tremendous effect on the day-to-day work of classroom teachers. Teachers may be asked to deliver on rigorous expectations and utilize new programs with very little time to learn the processes and resources behind them. The result can be emotionally taxing. "It is not change that causes anxiety; it is the feeling that we are without defenses in the presence of what we see as danger that causes anxiety" (Kegan & Lahey, 2009). While change may be inevitable, understanding how you experience change can be a first step in developing skills to respond and regain your confidence and control.

INDICATORS

- Heightened feelings of anxiety, such as persistent thought cycles around the demands of your work
- Confusion about what is expected of you to uphold expectations from your supervisor or colleagues
- Uncertainty about whether your work is having a positive effect

RESPONSIVE PRIORITIZATION STRATEGIES

1. Verify facts, avoid assumptions, and focus on your locus of control

It can be easy to become overwhelmed or anxious about the perceived or real expectations all around us. Developing a process to help filter information, correct inaccurate assumptions, and grasp what is truly within your realm of control can provide peace of mind, prompt reasonable action, and enhance your focus in a productive way. Practice using this simple activity once a week for several weeks to improve your ability to filter the daunting, overwhelming information around you into straightforward, manageable steps you can accomplish with ease!

Write a new story: First, sit down and write what is happening to you and around you at school this week. Include all possible details—who is involved, what is happening, how you feel, what you are thinking, and so forth.

Then, go through the story with a highlighter as if you were a news editor tasked to pull out *only* the facts in the story—highlight everything that is stated as if it were a fact. Use a pen to now cross out anything in the story that you cannot absolutely know to be true—judgments, assumptions, assignment of motive, bias, or premature conclusions.

Next, rewrite on a new sheet of paper only the facts that have survived your rigorous editing. You will be left with only the fact-based reality! Finally, categorize these facts according to Stephen Covey's Circles of Influence (S. R. Covey & Collins, 2020) that follows. Next to each item, write one of the following letters:

C: This item is within my direct *control*.

I: This item is not in my control, but I may be able to exert *influence*.

A: This item is not in my control, and I cannot influence it, but I can learn to *accept* it.

As you collect these analyses over several weeks, examine the trends and reflect:

- What are the sources of the items that surface as persistent concerns for me but that are out of my control and within my ability to influence?
- What action steps will I take toward influencing these areas in the next six months?

2. Develop your resilience

Resilience is the capacity to deal with change and continue to develop, bounce back, and be stronger. There are actions that explicitly cultivate the development of resilience and enable teachers to navigate change with optimism and agency. Research suggests that positivity is the secret to becoming resilient (Frederickson, 2009). Don't mistake positivity for blind optimism, however. As you approach a challenge, problem, or dilemma, consider the distinctions between deficit-based thinking (DBT) and asset-based thinking (ABT), developed by cognitive coaching consultant Lynn Sawyer (personal correspondence):

ASSET-BASED THINKING AND DEFICIT-BASED THINKING CHART

DEFICIT-BASED THINKING (DBT)	ASSET-BASED THINKING (ABT)
Not this again . . .	This can get better; I've seen this before.
That won't work!	What could work?
I'll never make it . . .	I'll take one step at a time.
That's impossible . . .	This will take a little longer than expected.
I've failed again!	What am I learning from each try?
They just don't get it!	We see this differently.

Resilience is the capacity to deal with change and continue to develop, bounce back, and be stronger.

Using the preceding statements, engage in the following self-reflection. This self-reflection is aimed at developing our positivity and, ultimately, our resilience to change:

- As I reflect on the last six months, what patterns am I noticing in my self-talk? Are they more closely aligned with DBT or ABT? What pattern strikes you as an area you would like to improve?

- What is the story I keep telling myself about the problems of this school/my students/my colleagues/my principal? What pieces of this story are based on fact, and what pieces are based on assumption?

- Now, what actions might I take to not only FEEL good but to add value to the world by DOING good?

PROBLEM: EXTERNAL PRESSURE TO ENGAGE IN A "HUSTLE CULTURE" OF OVERWORKING

ROOT CAUSE: FEAR OF MISSING OUT (FOMO) OR TOXIC PRODUCTIVITY

When feeling as though the calendar is overflowing and that prioritization is an unattainable feat, you may be experiencing the effects of toxic productivity. Toxic productivity is described as "an obsessive need to always be productive, regardless of the cost to your health, relationships, and life" (Neale, 2022). Teachers who engage in extraordinary amounts of work may do so because of internal or external drivers. Internal, personal influences can present as a passion, or drive, for being deeply involved in every aspect of the work. You might take on a leadership role in a PLC, volunteer to direct the school play, mentor a first-year teacher during your planning period, or perhaps all these things at once. The fear of missing out, often humorously referred to as FOMO, can elevate to dangerous levels, however. External influences on our productivity levels may present as social dynamics perpetuated by others. For example, silent judgment for leaving school at the day's end or withholding of affirmation by leaders for not being more of a "go getter." Teachers who experience toxic productivity may develop burnout or high stress from being overwhelmed, or they may not fulfill obligations as a result of overcommitting.

> **CONNECTION**
>
> - Read more about developing the habit of resilience in Chapter 10.

INDICATORS

- Frequently approached by others to join groups, engage in projects, pilot new initiatives, and so forth because you are a "yes!" person

- Presence of the "comparison monster," a self-talk practice in which you are rarely satisfied with your accomplishments and perseverate on the accomplishments of others

- Using your spare time to fulfill obligations for tasks or projects that aren't within your overall job description

> *Evan, a sixth-grade social studies teacher, was in his fifth year of teaching when the principal complimented him on his engagement in so many aspects of the school community. In a few years, he had helped lead the pilot of a new social-emotional learning*
>
> *(Continued)*

(SEL) curriculum at the school, become the chair of the social studies team at the middle school, and launched a new recycling program for the school with the student council he supervised. He beamed with pride at the principal's comment but winced—as he had just been talking to his husband about how his extensive commitment to school was impacting the amount of time he could spend at home with family. He couldn't possibly now tell his boss that he'd like to resign from some of his leadership positions. In fact, he was now even more inspired to apply for the District Teacher Advisory Committee he had learned about and leveraged this opportunity to ask his principal for the required recommendation letter.

RESPONSIVE PRIORITIZATION STRATEGIES

1. Zero in on your strengths

If you find yourself overwhelmed by your workload, recognize that you may also be feeling stressed because you are not adequately prepared to complete the tasks you committed to do. In the absence of appropriate capacity, you take on even more of a workload to learn how to accomplish the tasks at hand, thus wearing yourself down even further. Mitigate these experiences by committing only to new areas that align with your personal strengths or where you are striving to grow. For example, Evan tends to sign up for all requests. Meanwhile, he aspires to pursue his master's degree in Curriculum and Instruction and become a district curriculum director. Further, he's especially talented at leading others through long-term, complex projects (as he learned in the SEL curriculum pilot). Rather than taking every offer, this school year Evan plans to seek out projects related only to curriculum implementation and ask his principal to consider him for leadership positions in these groups.

2. Explore mindfulness strategies

Mindfulness practices and interventions have been proven to aid teachers in coping constructively with the demands of teaching (Beers & Skinner, 2016). In the book *Mindfulness for Teachers*, the author outlines specific benefits of mindfulness training, including increased understanding of your own emotions (Jennings, 2015). As you strive to regulate emotions that drive you to assume extraordinary levels of responsibility or that make you feel anxious at the prospect of disappointing others, mindfulness strategies provide an impactful entry point for improvement.

PROBLEM: UNCERTAINTY ABOUT THE FUTURE

ROOT CAUSE: LACK OF POSITIONAL AUTHORITY

Positional authority, or the ability to control your choices and influence change in your school, can be scarce for classroom teachers. When striving to prioritize how you spend your time, there will always be requirements placed on you by others—your team, your principal, the district, and so forth. You may feel as if your time is more dedicated to achieving someone else's goals than your own. Yet having agency over your situation is crucial to withstanding challenging experiences. Finding opportunities to develop your influence and control can be powerful antidotes! Begin by learning to reframe situations of power differentials to place yourself on the trajectory to success. You'll be empowered to identify actionable opportunities for altering your position toward one of confidence and influence.

INDICATORS

- Feelings of being unheard, unseen, or underappreciated

- Frequently receiving decisions from leaders or supervisors about which you had no input, involvement, or information

- Experiencing isolation within the staff community as a response to the absence of trust and mutual respect amongst team members

As Chanel entered her third year of teaching kindergarten, she was confronted with yet another work week where administrators sent a series of emails explaining new mandates for student behavior protocols, held meetings to share the updated requirements for lesson plan templates, and asked grade-level chairs to deliver details on new PLC protocol requirements. Wondering why she always felt as if she was just going through the motions with these compliance tasks, she noticed a fourth-grade teacher sharing the highlights of a committee meeting she attended. She spent some time talking to her colleague and learned that any teacher could participate in the advisory committee to elevate ideas and questions to the administration team. She asked the assistant principal, her direct supervisor, for a meeting to discuss this and other opportunities to become more involved in the decision-making processes at the school. Suddenly her outlook shifted from resigned and discouraged to optimistic and intrigued.

RESPONSIVE PRIORITIZATION STRATEGIES

1. Develop relationships and seek involvement opportunities

While you may feel as though your role as a classroom teacher does not come with the same opportunities to influence change as a principal, for example, your voice and ideas bring valuable insights to those leaders about improvement opportunities for the school! Begin developing your understanding of what possibilities are present for being a part of these conversations by observing, asking, and engaging.

Observe

- Who delivers the information to teachers about significant schoolwide initiatives or changes?
- Who, if anyone, has opportunities to contribute ideas when major changes are considered?
- Who participates in the leadership of implementing new initiatives or programs?

Ask

- What are the sources of impact on my schedule that feel like they are not within my control?
- How would I envision a scenario in which I had more autonomy and agency over my situation?
- Who can I connect with to develop a relationship and increase my understanding of how I may become a participant in the change processes in our school?

Engage

- Set informal meetings with those you identified as key influencers in your school to learn about their involvement and potentially find ways to join their efforts.
- Set a purposeful meeting with your administrator to indicate your interest in becoming a proactive participant in the direction of the school.
- Use the goal-setting strategies in Chapter 6 to focus personal effort on enhancing your feelings of autonomy.

2. Prioritize communication and self-advocacy

It may feel as though you are expected to be an instant expert at implementing new resources or strategies in the early phases. Perhaps those around you demonstrate calm confidence and easily put things into place. Yet it's perfectly normal to experience uncertainty or confusion when learning a new skill or practice. You may not be able to control the timeline required for the new phonics curriculum to be integrated into instruction, for example (see positional authority above), but you can improve your confidence in the process with simple, specific communication practices.

Seek and give clarity with all involved: In the process of learning a new strategy, skill, or resource, it's nearly impossible to process and apply everything at the speed with which it is shared, so there is a high chance you will miss key details. Gain clarity by:

- Asking questions the moment they arise. Send an email, ask a colleague, or write down your question to remember it when you have the attention of someone who can help.

- Verbalizing—by summarizing, paraphrasing, or restating— what it is you understand about the current requirements to someone who can confirm your knowledge.

Share progress updates periodically: It may seem as though your colleagues or supervisor wouldn't want to be inundated with mundane details about your completion of the training on the new assessment platform, but simply stating verbally or including in an email the fact that you are halfway through and will finish by Tuesday, for example, can be a value-add for others. For teammates, it may prompt them to realize they need to get going. For your leaders, it demonstrates that you are taking their expectations seriously, or conversely, that their demands were more intensive than they perceived and more time should be allocated. Regardless of the outcome, communication is always able to provide value to the progress of the overall initiative.

Self-advocate early and often: When deadlines are looming, supervisors likely spend little time wondering if they will be met or how things are going—they just want things to be accomplished. When the final hour arrives and suddenly urgent, anxious requests are presented for more time, their reaction is no different than yours to a student who procrastinated: concern and likely irritation. However, with clear communication of your needs—more time, extra support, and so forth—in advance of the completion deadline, they are empowered to collaborate with you and ensure your success. As you deepen your expertise at prioritization, you'll see ideal opportunities to practice self-advocacy and reap the rewards!

PROBLEM: TEACHERS ARE EXHAUSTED

ROOT CAUSE: DECISION FATIGUE

Decision fatigue is, as its name implies, mental exhaustion from constantly having to weigh options and make choices.

Teachers' days are often a flurry of swift, inconsequential decisions. Mixed in with those are weighty decisions around planning instruction or analyzing assessment results, however, a totality which can snowball you into decision fatigue. Every day presents a decision tree with infinite permutations and, without a specific plan created for how to allocate time to accomplish important priorities, it's easy to wander astray. We start to negotiate our responses to decisions that influence our improvement goals, and time whittles away. Faced with a question of whether you can make time to revise lesson plans based on formative assessment results, for example, you may shuffle other tasks, get distracted by emails, and ultimately make a rational trade-off: You won't review your plans today, but you will definitely be sure to do so next time. Conversely, when we proactively plan how our time will be spent around priorities, the decisions are already made and there is no thinking required when the moment arrives: We simply do what has been planned. As a result, energy can be focused where it is needed most, and our mind is able to respond agilely when distractions present themselves.

INDICATORS

- Analysis paralysis: Extensive time passing without accomplishing goals or completing tasks

- Apathy toward making any decisions at all as a result of feeling the outcomes are out of your control

- Frustration or heightened anxiety at the prospect of making any decisions

RESPONSIVE PRIORITIZATION STRATEGIES

1. Decision categorization

To understand why one might face decision fatigue, grab your favorite writing tool and spend ten minutes documenting every decision you made during your most recent planning period whether related to instruction or not. Next, write down one of two letters next to each line item: R or P.

- **R for reactive:** A decision you had not foreseen or for which you did not already have a plan in place

- **P for proactive:** A decision you knew would be approaching and for which you had already applied some planning

There is no perfect ratio of P to R, but if the majority of your decisions were under the reactive category, you may benefit from deeper learning in this chapter. Within the categorized list, start by selecting two to three R-labeled decisions that could have been planned for preemptively. Complete the following reflection guide to identify any patterns that can inform future decision-making.

REFLECTION

What was the decision about?

_____

_____

_____

Why did it become a "reactive" decision?

_____

_____

_____

What was the outcome of the decision you made?

_____

_____

_____

Who else was impacted by the this being a "reactive" decision?

_____

_____

_____

What is one action you will take to increase making future decisions proactively?

_____

_____

_____

As you develop prioritization skills, you will naturally improve your time management and find yourself better equipped to be proactive about daily decisions, thus freeing mental energy and preventing decision fatigue.

2. Write it down!

Organizing all of your information input is critical to effective short- and long-term planning. First and foremost, choose a tool for documenting goals, tasks, plans, and schedules that aligns with your most comfortable method of use: digital or analog (a printed calendar). Make space for short- and long-term planning, such as daily and weekly and semester or year. It is quite convenient to use daily "to do" lists, but if you aren't leveraging a planning tool to map out the sequence of steps needed to arrive at a long-term goal by a deadline, you're missing a crucial feature for prioritization.

You'll learn many more strategies around managing the calendar in the next chapter, but practice a first step of writing down your objectives for a school week using these steps:

1. **Plan for a Monday to Friday.** First, write down all the significant objectives (tasks, projects, goals, deadlines) you hope to accomplish by Friday afternoon, assuming that you will not spend time working over the weekend. Do not yet place any on the day of the week you think they will or should occur.

2. **Categorize the list** in order of how much time each objective is likely to require to accomplish, starting with the most demanding items at the top.

3. **Break down each item into action steps.** Attack each item one by one, beginning with the most time-demanding. Before moving onto the next item, place the different action steps for a single objective onto the different days of the week where you can confidently schedule time to complete them. Repeat this process until you move through the list. Important note: It's perfectly fine to realize you have too many objectives to fit in during this single week and move them to a future date. In fact, this is part of realizing how to be realistic with what you can actually accomplish to increase your success experiences!

4. **Complete this process for several consecutive weeks.** After at least three cycles, review your accomplishments and those items that didn't get completed. Use this data to inform your new planning cycle.

PROBLEM: TEACHERS DO NOT FEEL EMPOWERED

ROOT CAUSE: INITIATIVE OVERLOAD

Education has historically been a field where new initiatives are presented to teachers as the magical solution to our pressing issues. Whether driven by district changes, school improvement goals, or even an earnest colleague, these endeavors are often well intended. However, for a new curriculum, teaching practice, or any other variety of initiative to take hold and result in positive impact, there must be time to engage in skillful implementation. When multiple initiatives are adopted at once, this can place teachers in the precarious position of being asked to rapidly become proficient without fully understanding the purpose or value of the plan. The absence of clarity, time, and consistency may diminish teacher's agency and, ultimately, your ability to effectively prioritize those actions that will have the most impact on your students. Assessing the initiatives on your horizon and planning for how and when you will prioritize your attention to them is a first step toward successfully combatting initiative overload.

INDICATORS

- Spending significant time learning new practices, processes, or strategies

- Feelings of apprehension or distrust toward new ideas or resources

- Low confidence or even messy, disorganized implementation of new strategies and resources

RESPONSIVE PRIORITIZATION STRATEGIES

1. Conduct an initiative inventory

Navigating a maze of new curriculum to learn, technology apps, school schedules, or any number of things added to your "must do" list during the school year can seem daunting. Applying the specific prioritization strategies from *The Minimalist Teacher* (Musiowsky-Borneman & Arnold, 2021, p. 56) can provide structure, clarity, and focus:

1. **Inventory all current initiatives** (SEL curriculum, grading policies, etc.). Begin by documenting a list of new and existing initiatives that impact your daily work.

2. **Select one of the initiatives to conduct an analysis.** Choose one that is troublesome for you, one that you are passionate about, or one that is intriguing to you—any choice is fine!

3. **Pare the initiative down to its essentials** to ensure space and mental bandwidth for all the things you aspire to accomplish. Answer each of the following questions for the initiative you chose.

Purpose

- What value is this initiative going to add to what we already do?
- What role will I play in rolling out this initiative?

Priorities

- What are my priorities within this initiative?
- How will this initiative improve my teaching? Student learning?
- What is the timeline for implementation so I can take important steps between now and then to be prepared?

Pare Down

- What are the essential pieces of this initiative that I can build into what I am already doing?
- How can I set a structure to learn about this in an efficient way?
- What is the first step or key element I can start with?

4. **Repeat the analysis with each initiative you listed** and compare your results to begin synthesizing the information and developing a clear action plan.

2. Seek support!

In Chapter 2, you learned about the power of collaboration. Leveraging the power of teamwork can be crucial to success when it comes to learning new processes, determining the most valuable components of a new program, or accelerating your understanding of what is expected. Try any of these action steps to make the work lighter with the help of others:

- **Start a book study:** No, we don't mean to find a new book and add more to your plate. The "book" can be whatever resource or tool you are being asked to learn. Set a calendar of short meetings with several colleagues. Assign leadership roles to divide the work. Create focus questions for each meeting and come prepared to dig deep!

- **Peer review implementation plans:** With any new resource, you will certainly need time to plan for how it will come to life in the classroom. Don't suffer in silence—share plans with colleagues using the guiding questions in Chapter 7 on Using Feedback and be sure to cycle back for peer reflection after you roll out the new resource!

- **Schedule your action plan, celebrate your wins:** With everyone on staff undergoing the implementation process, take time early on to connect with colleagues and build a collective calendar for your progress. Whenever a deadline approaches, be sure to showcase everyone's accomplishments and recognize how hard the team is working.

- **Connect with your supervisor:** While sharing with a supervisor that you are experiencing overwhelm may feel like complaining, rest assured that they may have the ability to help! Setting up a conversation with a principal, for example, mitigates the presence of assumptions about why work may not be getting accomplished and enables them to support your needs. Be sure to visit the section on advocating for your needs in Chapter 7.

GETTING STARTED: BEGIN WITH WHAT MAKES SENSE

Learning or improving your prioritization skills is not something that requires a complete overhaul of existing habits. Different strategies may be more effective for some people than others, and there is no single solution that works every time. Like all habits, prioritization is a series of intentional actions that are acquired through diligent, repetitive practice. Recognize that each of the root causes previously described is a substantial experience in and of itself. When working on the responsive strategies described in this chapter, consider the following:

- Which root cause most resonates with your lived experience as a teacher?

- Which of these strategies connects most closely to the purpose you identified in Chapter 1 or the goals you developed in Chapter 6?

Using your answers, take time to employ the strategies associated with this root cause for a sustained period before moving on. For utmost long-term success in developing a sustained habit, be sure to reflect on your experience with each of the strategies. Use the reflection tool here as a guide to support your efforts.

Prioritization Reflection Guide

Root Cause of Focus:		
Strategy Practiced:	**Positive Outcomes:**	**Adjustments Needed for Future Success:**
Strategy Practiced:	**Positive Outcomes:**	**Adjustments Needed for Future Success:**

The Big Ideas

In Chapter 7, you learned the art of seeking and applying feedback toward reaching those goals you developed in Chapter 6. As you apply the practices and strategies presented in this chapter around prioritization, you're honing your skills at managing your time effectively and also progressing toward a state of personal and professional balance. Through the process of examining root causes that influence your ability to prioritize well, you learned what may be your most significant personal barrier to gaining confident control of your decision-making process! Use this chapter at regular intervals to continue testing each unique responsive prioritization strategy until you zero in on those that are most beneficial for you and your needs.

Let's Reflect

What are your most significant challenges when it comes to prioritizing your work? Areas of your personal life?

_____

_____

_____

Which of the responsive prioritization strategies will you utilize first? What outcome do you hope to achieve?

_____

_____

_____

What goals do you hope to accomplish by improving your skills in prioritization?

_____

_____

_____

What's Next?

Coming up in Chapter 9, you will dig into a common source of frustration and even burnout as a teacher: negativity. While seemingly a simple emotion to avoid, this chapter guides your focus toward proactively practicing habits that diminish the deteriorating effects of negativity. You will learn how using team norms, strategically applying responses to negativity, and proactively practicing positive actions can transform your daily emotional experiences.

CHAPTER 9

Avoid the Negativity

Randall, a new middle school teacher, was sitting eating his lunch in the teachers' lounge. Many of the teachers sat sipping on caffeine as it was the second month of school and exhaustion from kicking off the school year, completing the first round of report cards, and parent teacher conferences had set in. Difficult student behavior was also on the rise, and teachers were grumbling about their stress and exhaustion. Randall became very uncomfortable when the conversation became extremely negative. He found himself sitting and listening to his colleagues talk poorly about individual students. The conversation continued to become even more toxic when his colleagues started sharing their opinions on all the problems they had with their principal, school, and the district they were working in. The longer Randall sat in the lounge, the more uncomfortable he became. He did not share the same views, nor did he think it was mindful to be discussing the students' poor choices or these sensitive topics openly in the teachers' lounge. Randall later described the scenario and said it was like the teachers were in a competition to see whose class or students were the worst. The teachers had quickly spiraled into a carnival of complaints, instead of being mindful and respectful of their students, colleagues, and profession. Numerous comments around student motivation and lack of family support surfaced, and Randall left his lunch break feeling isolated and frustrated.

RECOGNIZING NEGATIVITY AND NAVIGATING PROFESSIONALLY

Negativity is contagious and can spread like wildfire. A "Negative Nellie/Ned" is a person with a toxic attitude that is negatively influencing other colleagues. Negative Nellies/Neds can be high performers, but their bad attitudes can influence and damage the culture and productivity of the rest of the team. Negative Nellies/Neds tend to be very outspoken in settings that undermine leadership and do not value all voices or the greater team. Furthermore, Negative Nellies/Neds tend to be constant complainers and see most of their life experiences through a pessimistic view. Gallup uses the term "actively disengaged" to describe Negative Nellies/Neds, or NNs, in their research. In 2018, Gallup research found that globally, there is almost a 1:1 ratio of engaged to actively disengaged employees within an organization. In short, the problem of NNs is very real and should be dealt with right away. Otherwise, the effect will be devastating to a team. (Ray, 2023)

In this chapter, we will discuss and reflect on various strategies and activities to help teachers orbit Negative Nellies/Neds within their teams or school. While negativity can spread like wildfire, the opposite is also true. Gratitude and a positive mindset are contagious and can shift the mindset of a team or school culture as well.

The challenge is how do you know whether someone (or even yourself) is acting like a NN or simply just needs to vent a little? This chart can be a useful tool.

A NEGATIVE NELLIE/NED IS . . .	A NEGATIVE NELLIE/NED IS NOT . . .
• A constant complainer	• Occasionally vents to appropriate individuals
• Has the "parking lot" meeting after a staff meeting to complain about people	• Occasionally vents in appropriate settings
• Frequently back channeling and triangulating with other teammates—in other words, talking about other team members without them present	• Ensures that all voices are heard, seen and valued
• Has a chronic bad attitude; one might frequently feel like walking on eggshells around them	• Has an occasional temporary bad attitude due to real life circumstances that are challenging
• Conversation trends around gossip about other people	• Conversation is focused on facts and procedures
• Has an armored personality, is not easy to approach, and easily finds fault in others	• Is approachable and provides a safe space for all voices to be heard; reflective about how they contributed to a problem
• Frequently blames others and does not reflect on their own attitude and the impact it has on those on their team	• Extremely reflective, owns when they make mistakes and seeks to improve the culture of their classroom, team, and school

With your grade-level team or individually, reflect and respond to the following questions.

REFLECTION

How has a negative or toxic attitude impacted your professional life in the past? Have you had any physical responses when interacting with the NNs (tight chest, high blood pressure, etc.)?

_____

_____

_____

How have you responded to the Negative Nellies/Neds in your past?

_____

_____

_____

What did you learn from those experiences that you wish you had done differently in navigating the NNs?

_____

_____

_____

NAVIGATING NEGATIVITY WITHIN YOUR TEAM THROUGH NORMS

In Chapter 5, we discussed the habit of using procedures and routines within the school and classroom, which can also be used to navigate the challenges of working with Negative Nellies/Neds. Procedures and routines have a positive impact on students' social and emotional wellbeing (Evenson, 2021). This same research also supports the use of procedures and routines to communicate effectively and efficiently with colleagues, thus positively impacting grade-level or content teams, professional learning communities, or staff meetings. When clear norms and procedures for communication are in place, it helps teammates orbit some of the challenges that they face when pessimistic or toxic mindsets and/or behaviors are present.

Taking time during a grade-level or content meeting to set norms and expectations is extremely valuable. Often teachers want to dive right into the content, schedule, data analysis, or student behavior supports. However, it is crucial that the team takes time to set norms and determine what hidden expectations might create challenges down the road.

Developing Team Norms Template

BRAINSTORM	REFLECTION
Reflect on the worst team experience you have ever had. Name the challenges you faced. Be as specific as possible.	(Example: Someone was rolling their eyes when a team member was talking.)
Share with your team the behaviors that created a challenge. Look for trends and write them down.	
Reflect on the best team experience you have ever had. Name the reasons or behaviors that created the positive team culture.	(Example: Teammates were always respectful of one another's time and started and ended meetings on time.)
Share with your team the behaviors that created a positive team culture. Look for trends and write them down.	
With these experiences in mind, discuss as a team what qualities make a good team experience versus a negative team experience.	

BRAINSTORM	REFLECTION
Considering the qualities the team named, identify the specific qualities that would contribute to the team's collective success and that everyone can adhere to.	
Determine as a team any "red flags" they potentially may have. Name the specific challenges or struggles and discuss them with all team members present.	(Example: Determining whether a virtual or in-person meeting would be most effective and efficient due to scheduling conflicts.)
Discuss and determine how the team will respond when someone is not following the agreed upon norms.	
Write up the norms and have them posted either electronically or on a table tent for everyone to see during future meetings.	
Determine who will start the meetings by quickly reviewing team norms. Ask, "Does anyone need clarification or need to check in on our norms?"	

NAVIGATING NEGATIVITY IN THE TEACHERS' LOUNGE OR COMMON SHARED SPACES

Most teachers' lounges are in open areas. This is important because it tends to be an area that many people have access to and where many people can listen to conversations teachers are having. While there is never a good space for teachers to complain or share stories about students, parents, or colleagues, the lounge historically has been a space that teachers tend to share more openly about the challenges of their day. Too often this conversation can turn into a competition of complaining. While teachers may see it as "their space" and feel they are venting to their colleagues, it is important to be mindful of the audience and professionalism and respect what is needed when sharing experiences.

Negative Nellies/Neds most often will park themselves in the teachers' lounge or gathering space and dive right into the carnival of complaints conversation. It is essential that teachers hold each other accountable and do not contribute to this tactic nor enable this behavior. Finding ways to either change the topic or confidently address the back channeling or gossip helps create a safe and welcoming culture for all staff and students. If the Negative Nellie/Ned becomes passive or overtly aggressive, simply removing yourself from the setting also works. Psychologists use the term "grey rock" to describe neutralizing interactions with toxic behaviors. "To grey rock a person involves making all interactions with them as uninteresting and unrewarding as possible. In general, this means giving short, straightforward answers to questions and hiding emotional reactions to the things a person says or does" (Villines, 2023). Negative Nellies/Neds are often seeking attention because they do not feel seen, valued, or heard. Chronic complaining is an attention-seeking behavior, and it is important to make those interactions as uninteresting or unrewarding as possible.

Here are some easy ways you can promote a positive atmosphere in the teachers' lounge and stay out of the weeds of negativity:

- **Trivia tables:** Intentionally place fun trivia cards at tables for teachers to interact with during their breaks.
- **Interactive bulletin boards:** Create an interactive bulletin board in the lounge to spark conversation or provide a brain break. A bulletin board with the theme "Would You Rather" sparks fun daily conversations through questions like, "Would You Rather" have a rewind button in life or a pause button in life? or "Would You Rather" be able to read people's minds or be invisible? Another bulletin board idea is to post a giant coloring poster and provide colored pencils or markers for staff to contribute to little by little.
- **Gratitude jars:** Using a simple jar and blank strips of paper, teachers can give "shout outs" of appreciation or gratitude to colleagues and school staff. During staff meetings,

someone can share out the contributions of gratitude. Negativity can spread like wildfire, but so can an attitude of gratitude! Being more thankful and appreciative brings more positive energy into the school culture. "According to the experts you can actually rewire your brain to focus on the positive, instead of looking for negative in every situation" (Vogel, 2023). The key is intentionally creating a space that fosters a positive work environment.

Use this template to brainstorm ways your grade level and school can intentionally focus on creating a positive space for your teachers' lounge.

ACTIVITIES OR IDEAS FOR ENGAGING STAFF	IDENTIFY A TEAM LEADER FROM EACH GRADE LEVEL TO BE THE ACTIVITY FACILITATOR. THIS PERSON IS COMMITTED TO ENGAGING OTHERS IN CREATIVE ACTIVITIES WHILE THEY ARE IN THE LOUNGE.
Staff kudos board	
Inspirational teacher or positive quote posters	
Monthly staff birthday bulletin board	
Teaching tidbit (teachers can share out powerful moves that are working)	
Joke of the week	
Gratitude jar and cards	
Trivia cards	

NAVIGATING ONE-ON-ONE CONVERSATIONS WITH NEGATIVE NELLIES AND NEDS

It can be easier to navigate conversations with Negative Nellies/Neds in a team setting rather than in one-on-one conversations. "Negative people can really bring you down, and it is extremely challenging to bring them up. For these negative people, something is always wrong. And to a positive person that becomes tiring quickly" (Evenson, 2021). In other words, spending your valuable time trying to cheer this person up one-on-one is often not helpful for you or them. Here are some conversation strategies you might consider:

- Develop routines that ensure others are around during common prep times, or make sure to take your break at a different time than them.

- Politely share with the Negative Nellie/Ned that negative conversation has been bringing you down lately and you are working on a personal goal to adopt a more positive mindset focused on gratitude.

- If you decide to lean in and have a more in-depth conversation with the Negative Nellie/Ned, make sure you have specific examples of things they have said and how that has made you feel. It is possible that the Negative Nellie/Ned will first deny they have acted this way or become defensive. You may not be able to change the Negative Nellie's/Ned's behavior through your conversation with them, as they may need professional support. Be prepared to offer empathy while setting clear boundaries that you are not able to engage in negative conversation with them any longer.

- Contact an instructional coach or administrator in your building to ask for tips on curbing negative conversations. The leadership team may already be aware of the negativity (so you don't have to name names), but you can seek out support in how to navigate the negative behaviors.

Find positive quotes to help ground you as you prepare to spend time with your learners. A great phrase to put near your desk is, "Ten minutes to eight, time to put on your tights and cape."

The most important thing is not to navigate this challenge alone. Remember to continue using gratitude throughout your own school day. Students need adults who can show up and be the best version of themselves. Building gratitude routines in your morning before students show up can help you greet your learners with a positive attitude.

If you choose to have a conversation with a Negative Nellie/Ned, use this reflection tool to prepare yourself for the conversation.

NEGATIVE COMMENT, SITUATION, OR ATTITUDE	HOW DID THAT MAKE YOU FEEL?

Consider role-playing this conversation with a friend or trusted colleague after you have written out the specific events you want to address.

NAVIGATING NEGATIVE NELLIES AND NEDS IN YOUR CLASSROOM

Up until this point, we have looked at Negative Nellies/Neds only as adults in a school building. However, students can display chronic negativity as well, which needs to be addressed. Effective classroom management is essential to achieve the goal of academic growth for all students. However, when students display disruptive and difficult behavior, it interferes with instructional growth and achievement. In Chapter 6, we examined how consistent and clear routines and procedures are extremely helpful when setting up classroom management and culture. This is especially true for students who may be anxious or have other social and emotional needs, as research shows they thrive in environments that are predictable (Korpershoek et al., 2016).

It is also important to recognize that after working with a difficult student, you may feel like you have exhausted your own bag of "tricks." Don't be afraid to ask for support from your peers, an instructional coach, or your principal about your current student challenges. A fresh set of eyes or collaboratively brainstorming ideas can be extremely helpful and lead to

CONNECTION

See Chapter 2 for more information about collaborating with peers and colleagues.

creative solutions. The most important part about seeking support from others is to remain neutral about how you feel about the learner and stick only to the challenging behaviors that you need to address. You don't want others to take on negative thoughts or perceptions about a student or a student's family based on how you speak about them/their family. Remember to provide your learner with the ability to start each day with a clean slate. This means you are mindful each day of your own frustrations and start with a clean slate as well.

As a result of the information you share with your leadership team, a positive intervention behavior plan can be created to help document and support the learner in your classroom. Your leadership team can advise you when to ignore negative behaviors and when to intervene. It is essential that we remember to navigate their behavior differently than a difficult adult or Negative Nellie/Ned. Ensuring that the learner is set up with the conditions of success daily may have significant impact on their learning and the learning environment they participate in.

Lastly, it is important to monitor your verbal and nonverbal communication when interacting with challenging behavior. Our tone and body language can signal to learners that we are either happy or frustrated. When working with challenging behaviors, it is crucial to remain neutral so that the students do not feed off our frustrations. Remain mindful of your tone, breathing patterns, and body language when working with challenging behaviors.

If you are feeling frustrated with a behavior, consider using the framework that follows to work through your own emotions and then help to reflect on a more desirable outcome for all stakeholders.

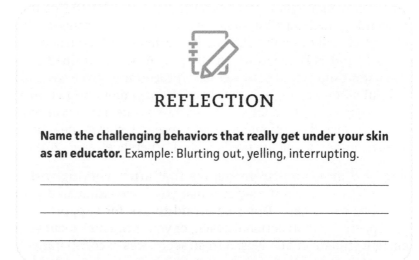

REFLECTION

Name the challenging behaviors that really get under your skin as an educator. Example: Blurting out, yelling, interrupting.

_____

_____

_____

What do you notice about your tone, breathing or body language when faced with these challenging behaviors? Example: Taking a deep breath and sighing.

_____

_____

_____

Is there a specific reaction you recognize you want to start working on to remain neutral when you face challenging behaviors in the class? Example: Work on shallow breathing and not sighing when faced with challenging behaviors.

_____

_____

_____

NAVIGATING NEGATIVE NELLIE/NED PARENTS AND CAREGIVERS

Communication certainly changed and yet, while there are more flexible forms of communication like email, social media platforms, communication apps, and the ability to meet virtually, the pressure and dynamics between families and schools seems to be more volatile. In other words, this may create tension in communication between both schools and families.

One factor that may be contributing to this is the open opportunity that social media platforms present for Negative Nellies/Neds to share their frustrations or vent. The risk and fear that at any point a parent, teacher, student, or principal can post whatever they are feeling or thinking has bred a culture of mistrust rather than a culture of teamwork where we collectively handle challenges through communication and collaboration toward the goal of student success. As such, it is important to be proactive and think of ways to make positive connections with families early in the relationship. With the support of an experienced colleague or instructional leader, reflect and proactively plan for how you want to build those positive connections with families. This is an important practice with all families but can be especially effective at warding off any potential Negative Nellie/Ned behaviors. For example, consider contacting all families via phone within the first few days of school and share something positive about their student. This creates a positive and open communication line right from the start and sets the tone for the school year.

CONNECTION

See Chapter 5 for more information on establishing effective routines and procedures with families.

In addition, when meeting with parents, whether virtually or in person, consider sharing positive traits of their learner prior to discussing any behavioral or academic challenges that may be occurring. Consider Franklin Covey's wise words of wisdom when working with a learner's parents, "Seek first to understand, then to be understood. Next to physical survival, the greatest thing a human being needs is psychological survival, to be understood, to be affirmed, to be validated, to be appreciated" (S. Covey, 2010). Make sure you enter this conversation with curiosity and humility, not with all the answers about the learner's disruptive behavior. Listen to the families and take notes of what their suggestions are about working with their students. This is a perfect opportunity to ask the parent or caregiver if they notice similar behaviors outside of school and, if so, what their suggestions are. Take to heart what the families say and their creative guidance.

If communication and interaction with a family becomes especially challenging, it is best to invite another educator or principal to any scheduled meetings. Just like you do not want to be alone with a colleague who is a Negative Nellie/Ned, the same theory applies here. Remember to lean on your experienced colleagues and instructional leaders in these difficult conversations because you do not need to handle them alone. Having another adult in a meeting to help facilitate the conversation is a powerful move or strategy.

NAVIGATING NEGATIVE NELLIE/NED SELF-TALK

CONNECTION

See Chapter 7 for more information about the importance of giving and receiving feedback.

Self-talk is the way we talk to ourselves, which is often called our inner voice. We may not be aware of our inner dialogue throughout the day, but the way you communicate with yourself is crucial and may be impacting your mental and emotional wellbeing. Our self-talk has the power to build up our confidence and empower us to work through challenging situations. But sometimes the critical way that we talk to ourselves can be self-destructive.

Everyone has moments of negative self-talk, but when we frequently surround ourselves with negative thoughts, it may have a harmful impact, especially when it comes to reflecting and providing feedback. We can easily be overly critical of ourselves, setting ourselves up for failure through unrealistic expectations.

Capturing your thoughts and reframing them is one strategy to help stop the cycle of chronically blaming and shaming ourselves. Whatever we practice repeatedly becomes ingrained in our mindset. Give yourself permission to pause and reflect on the narrative that is your current reality and the one that you want repeated in your mind. Use this chart to capture your thoughts and reframe what the Negative Nellie/Ned in your head is saying.

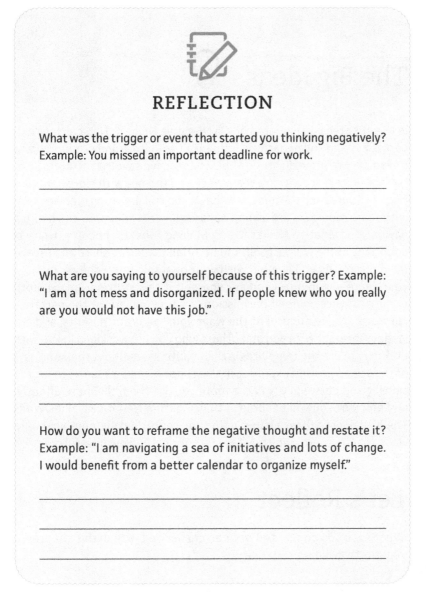

REFLECTION

What was the trigger or event that started you thinking negatively? Example: You missed an important deadline for work.

_____

_____

_____

What are you saying to yourself because of this trigger? Example: "I am a hot mess and disorganized. If people knew who you really are you would not have this job."

_____

_____

_____

How do you want to reframe the negative thought and restate it? Example: "I am navigating a sea of initiatives and lots of change. I would benefit from a better calendar to organize myself."

_____

_____

_____

After you capture your thoughts, put the reframed statement on a notecard or sticky note somewhere where you can read it several times a day. Capturing your thoughts and practicing positive thoughts repeatedly will help to rewire your thinking.

The goal is to notice what you are telling yourself and neutralize your negative thoughts so that you have the space to create a new, positive narrative in your head.

The goal is to notice what you are telling yourself and neutralize your negative thoughts so that you have the space to create a new, positive narrative in your head.

The Big Ideas

In this chapter, you explored how a Negative Nellie or Ned can be a high performer and still negatively influence the culture and productivity of a team. As we moved through this chapter, we saw that strategies for navigating toxicity within a team were also themes within previous habits. Procedures and routines, feedback, and collaboration (not isolation) with team members are all habits carefully threaded into the habit of navigating Negative Nellies/Neds. Moving forward, become aware or cognizant of the words, tone, and body language you share and receive from others. As you rumble with your own self-talk—the narrative in your head—be mindful and ask yourself if this information is helpful or hurtful? Give yourself permission to pause and adjust the narrative. Furthermore, be mindful of the ways your students, parents, and colleagues interact with you and others who you are working closely with. Continue to use the templates in this chapter throughout the year. Many of the strategies and exercises in this chapter can be used both professionally and personally, and the more you use them the more effective and efficient you will become with navigating Negative Nellies/Neds. The best way to form a habit is through repetition. Remember, habits wont change overnight; they take intentional and purposeful practice.

Let's Reflect

What have you connected or been challenged with in this chapter in regards to avoiding negativity?

_____

_____

_____

How do you want to contribute this upcoming year to supporting a positive school culture?

_____

_____

_____

When communicating with colleagues, students, and parents, is there an area such as tone, body language, or word choice that you want to set as a goal to improve in this year?

_____

_____

_____

What's Next?

In the next chapter, we will explore being adaptable. The habit of adaptability or flexibility is an essential throughline of our previous habits but will enable us to have strategies that further resiliency. As educators, it is essential for us to recognize the need for practicing adaptability or resiliency. Reframing negative thoughts to be more realistic and positive is not only a connection with the habit of avoiding negativity but also with the habit of adaptability or resilience. As you read the final habit, you will find that adaptability, like many of our previous habits, is a skill that can be developed, learned, and practiced.

CHAPTER 10

Putting It
All Together

Resilience Is Key

The quarter is drawing to a close at Hawthorn Elementary School and Henry, a second-grade teacher, finds himself walking into the third meeting of the week to plan—or rather, redo the original plan—for the upcoming professional development workshop he and his colleagues were asked to present to their teammates. Down the hall, his colleague rushes out of his room to begin basketball practice and lead the drills Henry was in charge of but will miss due to this meeting. Two other teachers were absent from the planning meeting that day, and Henry didn't have a chance to tell the principal that the event might be missing some elements if there wasn't enough time to prepare. He reflected on his feelings of satisfaction, however, that his students' recent performance task results on using arrays showed they had made tremendous progress since his observations of class discussions a week prior. At least something was going right, even if there still never seemed to be enough hours in a day to accomplish everything he felt needed to be done as an engaged member of the school staff.

RESILIENCE: MORE THAN JUST ACCEPTING INEVITABILITIES

It's no secret to a classroom teacher that flexibility is nearly equivalent to breathing in its utility to surviving the day-to-day journey in a school. Artfully designed instructional plans can be interrupted by unforeseen school picture makeup schedules, for instance, or global health issues could cataclysmically overtake entire school years (sound familiar? yeah, we thought so!). Countless education leaders and renowned experts have extolled to teachers the virtues of being flexible and adaptable. For some, it may have been the only guidance they could muster to support a field of professionals who faced colossal demands to fix unsolvable problems. Yet flexibility and adaptability have always been inherent characteristics— or intentional practices—of effective teachers. Together they comprise behaviors that are deeply rooted in a broader mindset of resilience or "the capacity to withstand or to recover quickly from difficulties" (Merriam-Webster, 2023). How teachers face change and navigate challenge and ambiguity encompasses sophisticated skills, which can and should be learned and refined as we grow in our professional journey. In fact, developing the ability to be resilient merits careful cultivation beyond simple encouraging words like "just roll with the punches" or "go with the flow."

The benefits of learning how to manage change and sustain confidence and control over our own wellbeing are more broadly defined through the American Psychological Association's definition of resilience (2023).

> The process of adapting well in the face of adversity, trauma, tragedy, threats and even significant sources of stress—such as family and relationship problems, serious health problems, or workplace and financial stresses.

UNDERSTANDING RESILIENCE

Resilience is multidimensional and transcends our personal and professional lives. Research suggests it is associated with increased job performance and satisfaction in a variety of professions (Avey et al., 2011). Resilience can be seen as the art of navigating challenge and change, and when a teacher is skilled in this area, they are less at risk for—though not impervious to—stress and burnout from sustained exposure to stress or repeated negative experiences (Mansfield et al., 2012). Resilience may have a tremendously positive impact on teachers' success and wellbeing overall.

Resilience has been found to be a crucial element in cultivating another mindset proven to positively impact our effectiveness as teachers: efficacy. Education researchers Hattie and Zierer (2018) define efficacy as, "The confidence or strength of belief that we have in ourselves that we can make our learning happen." In an environment of uncertainty, teachers may experience doubts about their impact or face anxiety from stress that negatively affects confidence and, therefore, efficacy. Fortunately, teachers are capable of learning to practice resilience in the face of change, constant chaos, fear, and doubt. By developing this skill as a habitual practice, teachers will not only protect but also build their sense of efficacy.

WHAT IT MEANS TO BE RESILIENT

Resilience is commonly associated with the ability to not only overcome a significant challenge or obstacle in life but to do so in a manner that results in positive growth in our social-emotional development. Further, resilient individuals may experience less impact from trauma than others with fewer coping skills as a result of applying factors of resilience throughout their daily life. For example, a resilient individual may have developed the ability to approach life with more optimism than someone who is less resilient, and they may have increased feelings that they can influence their destiny by leveraging factors within their control. When an unforeseen change occurs for a teacher, such as a sudden change of teaching assignment mid-year due to a colleague's resignation, a resilient teacher may certainly feel negative emotions such as discouragement or confusion. However, their capacity to adapt quickly to the change and see it as a learning opportunity comes from strength in resilience. Researchers Southwick and Charney (2018) describe ten factors contributing to an individual's resilience:

1. realistic optimism
2. facing fear
3. moral compass
4. religion or spirituality
5. social support
6. resilient role models
7. physical fitness
8. brain fitness
9. cognitive and emotional flexibility
10. meaning and purpose

CONNECTION

Several of these factors can be intentionally cultivated using activities and learning from prior chapters, such as "Clarify Your *Why*" (Chapter 1), "Prioritizing Amidst a Sea of Initiatives" (Chapter 8), and "Collaborate, Don't Isolate" (Chapter 2).

Although we don't examine each of these factors specifically within this book, it is important to recognize the unique areas around which your outlook on life and ability to navigate change and adversity can be developed throughout your career.

RESILIENCE IS . . .	RESILIENCE IS NOT . . .
• Viewing challenges as learning opportunities	• Believing that you will never have problems or face challenges
• Focusing on things that you can control instead of dwelling on what you cannot change	• Always having control or being in control of situations
• Reframing negative thoughts to be more realistic and positive	• Never experiencing negative emotions or thoughts
• A skill that can be developed, learned, and practiced	• Something you are either born with or without

NAVIGATING THE NEW ERA OF TEACHING: CHANGE AS A CONSTANT

What was once a career path associated with stability and longevity, contemporary teaching has evolved for many into a profession surrounded by constant ambiguity, change, and uncertainty. For example, as the world learns to coexist with widespread health pandemics that surge and dissipate with unpredictable intervals, schools are at risk of comprehensive changes to instructional delivery with abnormally short notice. The education workforce has experienced historically unprecedented rates of attrition at every level—from superintendents to classroom teachers. As a result, schools are subject to radical changes in leadership agendas around everything from curriculum to school calendars. Teachers who once may have stayed in the same school for most, if not all, of their careers may now migrate across different schools and districts, while yet other educators enter the profession to fill vacancies with non-traditional teaching backgrounds and/or emergency credentials. Change, without question, is the constant of the era, and teachers are compelled to learn to excel despite the absence of consistency.

Frequent change places teachers at risk for diminished confidence from being constantly in the novice or new phase of learning, whether around a new technology tool or something as critical as a comprehensive new reading curriculum. What were once trusted practices and routines for effectively teaching students who arrived in the fall with adequate proficiency in the skills and concepts for each prior grade level may fail to reach today's learners. It will be nearly 2040 before K–12 schools graduate the generation of children who were impacted by interrupted learning during the COVID-19 pandemic in some way. Our nation's economic and cultural diversity are distinctly more varied than at the onset of the twenty-first century as well, further dictating the need for ever-evolving education systems to adapt historic instructional practices in order to reach all children.

Teachers find themselves at the epicenter of societal changes that directly influence their daily work, and the field of education is overwhelmed with the message that a "quick fix" is urgently needed. It may feel as though you are being asked to achieve the impossible—or at least to tie yourself into metaphorical knots as an attempt to bend and flex in response to the demands from every direction. Amidst so much change, experiences of mastery—known to positively influence teachers' sense of efficacy—may be rare, causing diminished confidence and testing even the most resilient minds. Competency in content and pedagogy are crucial contributors to successful student outcomes, yet learning new strategies or processes takes time. Now, perhaps more than any other time in history, intentional development of resilience is essential to sustaining your wellbeing and ensuring your effectiveness as an educator.

APPLYING RESILIENCE
IN THE CLASSROOM

As you consider the role that resilience plays in your feelings of confidence and fulfillment as an educator, there are important implications for developing this mindset to ensure your utmost impact on student learning outcomes. For example, despite long hours of diligent effort designing rigorous, grade-level appropriate learning tasks, most of your students have not achieved the learning outcomes you intended. Suddenly, your confidence is in question, and you search for sources of explanation: students' prior learning gaps, the quality of your school's chosen curriculum, perhaps even the socioeconomic status of the families whose children attend your school. While it would require a research scientist to accurately determine the exact cause of students' unexpected performance, resiliency teaches us to focus on those areas that are within our control. Further, educator efficacy encourages us to embrace the belief that we are capable of implementing instructional strategies and effective practices that will mitigate, if not eliminate, the effects of the earlier detrimental factors we initially landed upon.

Here are some recommendations from a resilient educator, when asked about common classroom challenges.

SCENARIO	RECOMMENDATIONS FROM A RESILIENT EDUCATOR
You determine that instruction has fallen several weeks behind the pacing guide	Examine the pacing calendar and remaining days of instruction to determine areas of adjustment to ensure all standards are addressed.
	Collaborate with a more experienced colleague for ideas about how to prioritize instructional areas for the remainder of the year.
A guardian sends extremely negative, critical communication about the way you treat their child in class	Reflect on the root cause of the guardian's frustration before responding. Consider what areas are or are not within your control. Does the guardian have incomplete or misinformation?
	Seek feedback from a colleague or supervisor before responding.
	Recognize that you may not be able to resolve their concerns but acknowledge their opinions respectfully.
You absorb students from the class of a colleague who resigns midyear	Gather contact information for guardians of the students to welcome their children to your class.
	Collect and examine assessment data for the students and use it to determine students' academic readiness for current instruction.
	Seek support from administration. Collaborate around making decisions that meet your needs and the needs of the students.

SCENARIO	RECOMMENDATIONS FROM A RESILIENT EDUCATOR
You review student assessment results and observe downward-trending data, suggesting instruction isn't having the impact you expected	Compare data to grade-level or department peers to find classrooms where growth is occurring. Engage in peer observations of instruction. Seek support from instructional coaches or more experienced colleagues with purposeful planning for instruction.
You receive negative feedback from an administrator that conflicts with your understandings of effective teaching practices	Review the feedback received in a private setting, discerning key details of teaching practice mentioned. Seek additional visits from the administrator when you are implementing practices described in the observation for additional angles and settings for a complete picture of the concerns. Practice strategies in Chapter 5 for applying the feedback toward your professional growth.

REFLECTION

Now, consider what you have learned about resiliency. What characteristics of resilience do you see within the preceding educator responses?

_____

_____

_____

LEVERAGING EFFECTIVE HABITS TO BECOME A RESILIENT EDUCATOR

Throughout the chapters of this book, you have examined habits of personal and professional practice that contribute to your effectiveness as an educator, to your sense of self-efficacy, and to your ability to withstand the complex challenges faced every day in a school. Synthesizing the key learning from each chapter with what you have learned here about resilience, use this chart to reflect upon how each habit is likely to contribute to your personal development of resilience as an educator.

As with any skill, practice, or habit, it's important to recognize that when overly used, there may be a potential to diminish the intended positive effects. Use the "signals of overuse" column to reflect on what might happen if you applied this habit in a way that actually caused harm or prevented growth. Some of the reflection spaces are completed to help you generate initial ideas, but don't hesitate to add your own thoughts as well!

HABIT	CONTRIBUTES TO RESILIENCE BY ...	SIGNALS OF OVERUSE ...
Clarify your *why*		
Collaboration		Over-extending yourself to help others drains your time and energy, potentially even hurting your ability to be successful on projects
High expectations		
Using data to drive decisions		Overly interpreting data as an outcome of external factors that a teacher cannot influence (generational poverty, for example)
Procedures and routines		

HABIT	CONTRIBUTES TO RESILIENCE BY . . .	SIGNALS OF OVERUSE . . .
Setting goals		
Applying feedback		Gathering so much feedback that decisions become overwhelming, even paralyzing, thus diminishing confidence
Prioritization and decision-making	Focusing your work using specific organization strategies empowers you to control your schedule and achieve expectations, thus building hope and confidence	
Avoiding negativity		

BUILDING YOUR PSYCHOLOGICAL CAPITAL

Psychological capital is our ability to use our mental resources to help us get through difficult situations. As you develop connections between resilience factors and your ability to thrive throughout your career as a teacher, recognize that you are actively building your own psychological capital. You are investing in your ability to sustain any challenge you face, no matter how large. Together, resilience and efficacy contribute to your comprehensive bank of psychological capital, a contemporary term for a collection of skills that research suggest can be proactively developed to nurture thriving, happy individuals and organizations (Avey et al., 2011). The other two factors comprising psychological capital are hope and optimism (Luthans et al., 2015). As you begin to read this section of the chapter, reflect on the following question.

REFLECTION

Why might it be important to shift the focus to happiness in one's life, as well as how we examine the roles we assume in our school community?

_____

_____

_____

PROACTIVELY DEVELOP YOUR INNER H.E.R.O

Among other areas (e.g., creativity, courage, or mindfulness), positive psychology is the compilation of four major mindsets: hope, efficacy, resilience, and optimism. Together they comprise the acronym H.E.R.O. While you may possess varying degrees of each of these mindsets already, you will most certainly find that they vary and change fluidly throughout your career and in different experiences. However, as you strive to master the art of thriving amidst any environment or setting in which you find yourself as a teacher, each of these areas is a set of skills that can be intentionally practiced and developed, just as we have been learning in the prior pages around resilience. Let's begin by adding conceptual understandings of _hope_ and _optimism_ to those we have developed for _resilience_ and _efficacy_:

> **Hope** is commonly confused with wishful thinking (Lopez, 2013), unsubstantiated positive thinking, or even an illusion. Luthans et al. (2015) described the positive psychology framework of hope as deriving from "a cognitive or 'thinking' state in which an individual is capable of setting realistic but challenging goals and expectations, and then reaching out for those aims through a self-directed determination, energy, and perception of internalized control." Do you notice the association of hope with agency and internalized control? Hope is closely

linked to efficacy and reflects a belief that you possess both the will and the way to achieve your goals.

Optimism is commonly understood as the belief that positive outcomes will occur (Luthans et al., 2015). You may believe that you are either an optimistic person or a pessimistic person based on your general outlook on life and patterns in your responses to different scenarios, but it is not solely about disposition. Optimism can easily present as a form of self-confidence, though the two are not always linked. Researchers describe optimism as an explanatory style (Seligman, 1998). "An optimist attributes positive events to personal, permanent, and pervasive causes and interprets negative events in terms of external, temporary, and situation-specific factors" (Luthans et al., 2015, p. 118). As a teacher, you might demonstrate optimism when you believe you were awarded a leadership role because of your inherent strengths and hard work, whereas a pessimist may believe it was just good luck or a lack of other qualified candidates. Optimists also tend to believe they have a reasonable amount of control over most situations, regardless if that perception is accurate.

Along with resilience and efficacy, hope and optimism can also be developed and cultivated to contribute to your overall psychological capital. The theory of psychological capital asserts that these four factors contribute to positive psychology, or an approach toward all kinds of situations and circumstances that "positively oriented human resource strengths and psychological capacities can be measured, developed, and effectively managed for performance improvement in today's workplace" (Luthans, 2002, p. 59).

STRATEGIES FOR DEVELOPING YOUR H.E.R.O

Consider this bank of practical strategies you might utilize to develop each of the components of H.E.R.O in your classroom or beyond. Practice adding additional ideas of your own.

TO DEVELOP HOPE I CAN . . .	TO DEVELOP EFFICACY I CAN . . .
• Set goals *toward something* (tasks, emotional states, etc.) using strategies from Chapter 6.	• Before attempting something new or challenging, focus on identifying past successes or mastery experiences.
• Identify your motivation sources and develop plans to engage with them more consistently.	• In the case of negative experiences, practice reframing their outcome as something positive.

(Continued)

TO DEVELOP RESILIENCE I CAN . . .	TO DEVELOP OPTIMISM I CAN . . .
• Try new strategies to solve problems. Improvise! Journal around the experience and the outcome.	• Collect some data! Reflect on your response patterns to different situations at work (To what do you attribute events and interactions occurring?).
• Practice identifying your purpose using strategies in Chapter 1, and revisit your purpose whenever faced with a challenge or obstacle.	• Practice strategically shifting your response in future experiences and reflect on the change outcome.

PRACTICE APPLYING H.E.R.O

Erin has been working at the same school for eight years. This year, she faced immense challenges developing strong relationships with her students. In fact, she was very frustrated with herself for having to send so many students to the office for discipline support. She'd never had to rely on the administration so much before. It's summer break, but she can't help worrying, as she has heard the students coming to the grade next fall are quite a handful, too . . .

REFLECTION

What is/are the source(s) of Erin's negativity?

_____

_____

_____

Describe how each specific aspect of H.E.R.O. might be helpful for Erin to cultivate?

Hope	
Efficacy	

Resilience	
Optimism	

What are the first next steps you would recommend for Erin?

_____

_____

_____

Journal a recent school or classroom experience that caused you to feel increased stress, anxiety, pressure, or frustration.

_____

_____

_____

Now, use the H.E.R.O. guide to reflect on how you might respond to this challenging experience.

HOPE: I am hopeful that the outcome of this situation will lead to the positive change of . . .	
EFFICACY: While this is a difficult or challenging experience, I know I possess skills to navigate it, including . . .	
RESILIENCE: Even though I'm unhappy or uncomfortable in this situation or I find it to be challenging, I will focus my actions around demonstrating my personal values and stay true to myself. Some values guiding my actions include the following:	
OPTIMISM: This challenging situation isn't easy! However, I will gather some data to determine if it's as bad as it seems. Reflecting on the data that I gathered, I learned . . .	

MAKE THE JOB YOU HAVE
THE PROFESSION YOU LOVE

Another strategy developed by positive psychology researchers is known as job crafting. Job crafting (Wrzesniewski & Dutton, 2001) involves altering the framework of your job to make it more meaningful. The best part is that it is entirely guided by you, the teacher, and not your supervisor. Job crafting entails taking time to document and sort, or organize, various features of your job: tasks, schedules, relationships, and purpose. You may have already created resources that will influence a job crafting activity—for example, when you examined your "why" in Chapter 1 or organized your priorities and decision-making processes in Chapter 7. Further, determining areas of your work over which you have control or ways in which you can set goals toward improvement can also be leveraged within job crafting. Three major areas guide a simple structure of job crafting (Wrzesniewski & Dutton, 2001):

1. **Task crafting:** changing the number, scope, or type of job tasks

2. **Relational crafting:** changing the quality and/or amount of interaction with others encountered in your daily work

3. **Cognitive crafting:** changing the way we perceive our work

Consider examples of each of these areas as they pertain to classroom teachers.

	FIRST ACTION STEP	DEVELOPMENT ACTIONS
Task Crafting	Document the different ways in which you spend your time in a school day and within a school week. Use larger squares/circles for more time and smaller squares/circles for less to create a visual representation.	Move the colored shapes you created for cognitive crafting to discern relationships between how much time you spend on tasks that align with your purpose.
Relational Crafting	Document the important (or frequently present) people in your work. Denote key descriptors next to their name based on how they influence you. Do they support you? Distract you? Make you better? Discourage you? **Hint:** Look back at your Negative Nellies/Neds for more on this topic!	Draw lines between the individuals you identified and what tasks they commonly engage in alongside you.

	FIRST ACTION STEP	DEVELOPMENT ACTIONS
Cognitive Crafting	Brainstorm your motives, strengths, and passions. Create colored icons (squares, circles, etc.) to represent these areas. Consider addressing the following: 1. What keeps you engaged at work? 2. Why do you stay in teaching? 3. What inspires you to work harder or persist despite obstacles? **Hint:** Use your activities in Chapter 1 for this step.	Move the names of individuals to the colored circles based on whether they fuel your ability to achieve your purpose.

As you complete the diagrams, apply the reflection tool that follows to guide your next steps for proactively making changes that will enhance your new job framework. As with anything new, it will take time and consistent practice to experience the positive impacts of the change so be patient and persistent! Refer back to your job diagram often for updates, revisions, or reflections on the outcomes of your changes.

REFLECTION

What surprised you about the job crafting activity? Why do you think that is the case?

_____

_____

_____

What do you believe will be the most impactful change you may make as a result of the job crafting activity? Why?

_____

_____

_____

(Continued)

(Continued)

How does the job crafting activity relate to your journey toward developing hope, efficacy, resilience, and optimism about teaching?

_____

_____

_____

The Big Ideas

In this final chapter, you examined the opportunity to improve your wellbeing as a teacher through cultivating resilience, a mindset that transcends both your personal and professional lives and supports your success in practicing each of the habits described in this book. Digging into the concepts of H.E.R.O. (hope, efficacy, resilience, and optimism) ideally sheds light on mindsets and practices that you may proactively learn and apply. Recognizing your own agency in this journey to drive development in these areas supports not only you but your students' wellbeing as well. As students learn in classrooms with teachers who are confident in navigating ambiguity and change, they, too, are enabled to become more competent in these areas. Through the activities around "job crafting," you may see opportunities to link your purpose developed in Chapter 1 to specific goals you established in Chapter 6, thus leveraging the habits across different areas to maximize your growth and success. Where relevant, consider utilizing your collaboration skills from Chapter 2 to support fellow educators in their pursuit of feeling fulfilled and inspired as an educator. Chapter 10 is the ideal resource for pairing with each of the other habits as you grow and thrive in your career.

Let's Reflect

In what ways does your ability to develop hope, efficacy, resilience, and optimism affect learning outcomes for your students?

_____

_____

_____

What are the differences and/or similarities between your current beliefs about resilience and those you held when you first began teaching?

_____

_____

_____

How do you envision resilience connecting to your development of confidence across each of the other habits in this book?

_____

_____

_____

What's Next?

As the book comes to close, take time to reflect on your specific learning within this chapter using the preceding reflection questions. Read the conclusion as a reminder of how these habits work together to build a resilient educator, and set your action steps for moving forward in your learning.

Epilogue

As educators ourselves, we set out to write this book because we watched the educational landscape change for leaders, teachers, students, and families. We felt a sense of overwhelm as we watched the pressure and climate that comes with change. We were in constant conversations about the teaching shortage as we continued to watch thousands of educators leave the profession. Due to the swift changes in education, some of the schools we were supporting at the inception of this book were missing a third of their staff. We were supporting new and veteran teams of teachers that were expected to jump in and create classroom cultures that promote vulnerable and safe places for rigorous academic learning. However, we noticed that some habits that create these learning environments were not taught in undergraduate teacher education programs, and many teachers who were enrolled in education programs or began their first year of teaching during the COVID-19 pandemic were missing crucial in-person instructional training experiences. As a result, we noticed new and veteran teachers needing practical and sustainable habits that would support the conditions of success to establish classroom cultures that promote readers, writers, and thinkers. These research-based habits that educators need to be resilient and thrive during times of anxiety, doubt, and constant change are shown in the following figure.

By building up these effective and resilient habits, we can shift the narrative around hopelessness and overwhelm many educators are continuing to feel. Our aspiration is that when you purposely practice each habit, you will be able to feel more confident during times of ambiguity, uncertainty, and volatility and be able to focus on far more important and cognitively demanding priorities—such as standard-based instruction and assessment of student learning. While all nine habits are equally important and should be developed over time, our desire is that after reading the book, you will be inspired to identify one or two habits to focus on first and use the interactive reflection activities within those chapters to engage more deeply with the content and plan intentionally to apply your learning. These habits are catalysts for continuously improving your profession or craft as a teacher and should be practiced daily.

SPREADING RESILIENT HABITS

Every student needs a passionate and equipped teacher. Technology has become a terrific resource to support academic growth and achievement. However, as Chase Nordengren states, "No amount of technological innovation or structural change will eliminate the need for learning directed by caring, knowledgeable adults" (Nordengren, 2022, p. 117). In a contemporary teaching environment filled with stresses, teaching has become even more overwhelming and challenging. Now more than ever teachers and students need to develop habits of resiliency so that both the science and art of teaching benefits the academic and social-emotional growth and achievement of all students.

We know you can do this work on your own, but remember the power of collective teacher efficacy. Building habits of resilient educators is more fun and can have a greater impact when done with others. We are better together and must commit to practicing the resilient habits of teaching to regain control of our mindset amidst the chaos we face. The research-proven habits described in this book focus on creating a positive and supportive network of influences that can spread across a grade level, a department, or even an entire school.

When these habits are routinely practiced individually or with colleagues, they become optimal effective and efficient patterns in your personal and professional life. For example, consider inviting colleagues to focus on one resilient habit a month with you. Frequently set goals around improving a specific habit. Give yourself permission to revisit a chapter and continue to reflect and refine each habit as you see specific needs in your personal and professional life pop up.

At the beginning of this book, you created your own learning intentions. As we conclude our journey together, let's revisit those learning intentions and revise them as you continue to prioritize being open, curious, and receptive to practicing the resilient professional and personal habits of effective educators.

MY LEARNING INTENTIONS AT THE CONCLUSION OF THIS BOOK ARE . . .

1.

2.

3.

References

American Psychological Association. (2023). Resilience. *APA Dictionary of Psychology*. Retrieved October 2, 2023 from https://dictionary.apa.org/resilience

Aronson, B. (2017). The white savior industrial complex: A cultural studies analysis of a teacher educator, savior film, and future teachers. *Journal of Critical Thought and Praxis, 6*(3), 36–54.

Avey, J. B., Reichard, R. J., Luthans, F., & Mhatre, K. H. (2011). Meta-analysis of the impact of positive psychological capital on employee attitudes, behaviors, and performance. *Human Resource Development Quarterly, 22*(2), 127–152. https://doi.org/10.1002/hrdq.20070

Baker, K. (2020). *Wake up and spill the coffee: How I woke up to deficit ideology*. NWEA. https://www.nwea.org/blog/2020/wake-up-and-spill-the-coffee-how-i-woke-up-to-deficit-ideology/

Bandura, A. (1997). *Self-efficacy: The exercise of control*. Worth Publishers.

Beers, J., & Skinner, E. (2016). *Mindfulness and teachers' coping in the classroom: A developmental model of teacher stress, coping, and everyday resilience*. https://doi.org/10.1007/978-1-4939-3506-2_7

Boaler, J. (2015). *Mathematical mindsets*. Jossey-Bass.

Brown, B. (2018). *Dare to lead*. Vermilion.

Capizzi, A. M. (2009). Start the year off right: Designing and evaluating a supportive classroom management plan. *Focus on Exceptional Children, 42*(3), 1–12.

Clarke, S. (2021). What's so important about learning intentions and success criteria? Corwin-connect.com. https://corwin-connect.com/2021/06/whats-so-important-about-learning-intentions-and-success-criteria/

Clear, J. (2018). *Atomic habits. An easy & proven way to build good habits & break bad ones*. Avery.

Covey, S. (2010). *The 7 habits of highly effective people*. Simon & Schuster.

Covey, S. R., & Collins, J. C. (2020). *The 7 habits of highly effective people: Powerful lessons in personal change*. Simon & Schuster.

Dampf, E. (2022, October 1). It's about skillsets and support, not sainthood. *ASCD, 80*(2). https://www.ascd.org/el/articles/its-about-skillsets-and-support-not-sainthood

Danielson, C. (2013). *Enhancing professional practice: A framework for teaching* (3rd ed.). Association for Supervision and Curriculum Development.

Dewey, J. (1913). *Interest and effort in education*. Houghton Mifflin.

Dweck, C. (2023, March 27). *Carol Dweck revisits the "growth mindset" (opinion)*. Education Week. https://www.edweek.org/leadership/opinion-carol-dweck-revisits-the-growth-mindset/2015/09

Dweck, C. (2016). *Mindset: The new psychology of success*. Ballantine Books.

Eggleston, J. (2019). *Teacher decision-making in the classroom: A collection of papers*. Routledge.

Ellerbrock, C. R., Abbas, B., Dicicco, M., Denmon, J. M., Sabella, L., & Hart, J. (2015). Relationships—The fundamental R in education. *Phi Delta Kappan, 96*(8), 48–51. https://kappanonline.org/relationships-fundamental-education-ellerbrock/

Evenson, R. (2021, September 13). *12 powerful ways to deal with negative coworkers*. Harper Collins Leadership Essentials. https://hcleadershipessentials.com/blogs/relationships-and-communication/12-powerful-ways-to-deal-with-negative-coworkers

Fisher, D., & Frey, N. (2019). *PLC+: Better decisions and greater impact by design*. Corwin.

Frederickson, B. (2009). *Positivity: Top-notch research reveals the 3-to-1 ratio that will change your life.* Harmony.

Frey, N., & Fisher, D. (2022, March 1). *Are you communicating high expectations?* ASCD. https://www.ascd.org/el/articles/are-you-communicating-high-expectations

Garet, M. S., Wayne, A. J., Brown, S., Rickles, J., Song, M., & Manzeske, D. (2017). *The impact of providing performance feedback to teachers and principals, executive summary* (NCEE 2018-4000). National Center for Education Evaluation and Regional Assistance, Institute of Education Sciences, U.S. Department of Education.

Goddard, R., Hoy, W., & Hoy, A. (2004). Collective efficacy beliefs: Theoretical developments, empirical evidence, and future directions. *AERA, 33*(3), 3–13.

Gorski, P., & Swalwell, K. (2023). *Fix injustice, not kids and other principles for transformative equity leadership.* Association for Supervision and Curriculum Development.

Greenberg, M. T., Domitrovich, C. E., Weissberg, R. P., & Durlak, J. A. (2017). Social and emotional learning as a public health approach to education. *The Future of Children, 27*(1), 13–32. http://www.jstor.org/stable/44219019

Grinder, M. (2023). *What is nonverbal communication and why it's important: Examples, tips and more.* Michael Grinder & Associates. https://michaelgrinder.com/non-verbal-communication/

Hammond, Z. (2014). *Culturally responsive teaching and the brain: Promoting authentic engagement and rigor among culturally and linguistically diverse students* (1st ed.). Corwin.

Hart, H., Young, C., Chen, A., Zou, A., & Allensworth, E. M. (2020). *Supporting school improvement: Early findings from reexamination of the 5essentials survey.* University of Chicago Consortium on School Research.

Hattie, J. (2021a). *Collective student efficacy: Developing independent and interdependent learners.* Corwin.

Hattie, J. (2021b). *Visible learning metax* [Database]. https://www.visiblelearningmetax.com/

Hattie, J. A. C., & Zierer, K. (2018). *Ten mindframes for visible learning: Teaching for success.* Routledge.

Hubbard, F. (2023). *The equity expression: 6 entry points for nonnegotiable academic success.* Corwin.

Intuit. (2022). *The 20 most fulfilling jobs + the psychology behind them.* Mint.com. https://mint.intuit.com/blog/career/most-fulfilling-jobs/#entry-content

Jennings, P. (2015). *Mindfulness for teachers: Simple skills for peace and productivity in the classroom.* W. W. Norton & Company.

Kegan, R., & Lahey, L. (2009). *Immunity to change: How to overcome it and unlock the potential in yourself and your organization.* Harvard Business Review Press.

Keller, H. (1933, February). *Letter to president hoover from Helen Keller* (February, 1933, copy). The American Foundation for the Blind. https://www.afb.org/about-afb/history/helen-keller/letters/herbert-hoover

Korpershoek, H., Harms, T., de Boer, H., van Kuijk, M., & Doolaard, S. (2016). A meta-analysis of the effects of classroom management strategies and classroom management programs on students' academic, behavioral, emotional, and motivational outcomes. *Review of Educational Research, 86*(3), 643–680. https://doi.org/10.3102/0034654315626799

Kraft, M. A., Blazar, D., & Hogan, D. (2017). The effect of teacher coaching on instruction and achievement: A meta-analysis of the causal evidence. *Review of Educational Research, 88*(4), 547–588.

Lester, R. R., Allanson, P. B., & Notar, C. E. (2017, November 30). *Routines are the foundation of classroom management.* Education. https://eric.ed.gov/?id=EJ1144313

Lopez, S. (2013). *Making hope happen.* Atria.

Luthans, F. (2002). The need for and meaning of positive organization behavior.

Journal of Organizational Behavior, 23(6), 695–706. https://doi.org/10.1002/job.165

Luthans, F., Youseff-Morgan, C., & Avolio, B. (2015). *Psychological capital and beyond.* Oxford University Press.

Mansfield, C. F., Beltman, S., Price, A., & McConney, A. (2012). "Don't sweat the small stuff:" Understanding teacher resilience at the chalkface. *Teaching and Teacher Education, 28*(3), 357–367. https://doi.org/10.1016/j.tate.2011.11.001

Markus, D. (2023, August). The power of words. *Psychology Today.* https://www.psychologytoday.com/us/blog/designs-strong-minds/202208/the-power-words

Marzano, J. M. (2009). *Designing and teaching learning goals and objectives: Classroom strategies that work.* Marzano Research Laboratory.

McCarty, C., Redmond, P., & Peel, K. (2021). Teacher decision-making in the classroom: The influence of cognitive load and teacher affect. *Journal of Education for Teaching: International Research and Pedagogy, 47*(4), 548–561.

Merriam-Webster. (2023). Habit. In *Merriam-Webster.com* dictionary. Retrieved September 27, 2023, from https://www.merriam-webster.com/dictionary/habit

Merriam-Webster. (2023). Resilience. In *Merriam-Webster.com* dictionary. Retrieved September 27, 2023, from https://www.merriam-webster.com/dictionary/resilience

Milner, H. R., Cunningham, H. B., Delale-O'Connor, L., & Kestenberg, E. G. (2019). *"These kids are out of control": Why we must reimagine "classroom management" for equity.* Corwin.

Musiowsky-Borneman, T., & Arnold, C. Y. (2021). *The minimalist teacher.* Association for Supervision and Curriculum Development.

National School Reform Faculty. (2022, March 30). *What is a critical friends group?* National School Reform Faculty. https://nsrfharmony.org/faq-items/cfgvsplc/

Neale, P. (2022, January 22). When doing is your undoing: Toxic productivity. *Psychology Today.* https://www.psychologytoday.com/us/blog/leading-success/202201/when-doing-is-your-undoing-toxic-productivity

Nelsestuen, K., & Smith, J. (2020, October). Empathy interviews. *The Learning Professional, 41*(5), 59. https://learningforward.org/wp-content/uploads/2020/10/tool-empathy-interviews.pdf

Nordengren, C. (2022). *Step into student goal setting: A path to growth, motivation, and agency.* Corwin.

NWEA. (n.d.). *Culture of inquiry.* Professional Learning Seminar. https://www.nwea.org/school-improvement/school-improvement-professional-learning/

Oakes, A. (2015, September). *Family-school partnerships: 9 beliefs and attitudes for success.* Institute for student achievement. https://www.studentachievement.org/9-beliefs-and-attitudes-that-foster-collaborative-family-school-partnerships/

Ray, J. (2023, June 20). *Americans' stress, worry and anger intensified in 2018.* Gallup.com. https://news.gallup.com/poll/249098/americans-stress-worry-anger-intensified-2018.aspx

Rincon-Gallardo, S., & Fullan, M. (2016). Essential features of effective networks in education. *Journal of Professional Capital and Community, 1*(1), 5–22.

Sabbott. (2013, December 13). *Backward design definition.* The Glossary of Education Reform. https://www.edglossary.org/backward-design/

Samuels, C. A. (2020, November 19). *Greatschools' ratings revamp credits schools for boosting academic growth.* Education Week. https://www.edweek.org/policy-politics/greatschools-ratings-revamp-credits-schools-for-boosting-academic-growth/2020/09

Schaefer, S., Morozink, B., van Reekum, C., Lapate, R. C., Norris, C. J., Ryff, C. D., & Davidson, R. J. (2013). Purpose in life predicts better emotional recovery from negative stimuli. *PLoS One, 8*(11), e80329

Scheeler, M. C., Ruhl, K. L., & McAfee, J. K. (2004). Providing performance feedback to teachers: A review. *Teacher Education and Special Education, 27*(4), 396–407.

Seligman, M. E. P. (1998). The prediction and prevention of depression. In D. K. Routh & R. J. DeRubeis (Eds.), *The science of clinical psychology: Accomplishments and future directions* (pp. 201–214). American Psychological Association. https://doi.org/10.1037/10280-008

Southwick, S., & Charney, D. (2018). *Resilience: The science of mastering life's greatest challenges* (2nd ed.). Cambridge University Press.

Stronge, J. H., & Grant, L. W. (2014). *Student achievement goal setting.* Routledge. https://doi.org/10.4324/9781315854953

Toom, A., Pyhalto, K., & Rust, F. O. (2015). Teachers' professional agency in contradictory times. *Teachers and Teaching Theory and Practice, 21*(6), 615–623.

Villines, Z. (2023, January 10). *Grey rock method: What it is and how to use it effectively.* Medical News Today. https://www.medicalnewstoday.com/articles/grey-rock

Vogel, K. (2023, February 11). *Cultivating an "Attitude of Gratitude" can vastly improve your life—Here's how to do it.* https://parade.com/1223325/kaitlin-vogel/attitude-of-gratitude/

Vos, J., & Vitali, D. (2018). The effects of psychological meaning-centered therapies on quality of life and psychological stress: A metanalysis. *Palliative & Supportive Care, 16*(5), 608–632.

Wellman, B., & Lipton, L. (2017). *Data-driven dialogue: A facilitator's guide to collaborative inquiry.* MiraVia.

Wisniewski, B., Zierer, K., & Hattie, J. (2020). The power of feedback revisited: A meta analysis of educational feedback research. *Frontiers in Psychology, 10,* 3087. https://www.frontiersin.org/article/10.3389/fpsyg.2019.03087

Wrzesniewski, A., & Dutton, J. (2001). Crafting a job: Employees as active crafters of their work. *The Academy of Management Review, 26*(2), 179–201.

Zee, M., & Koomen, H. M. (2016). Teacher self-efficacy and its effects on classroom processes, student academic adjustment, and teacher well-being: A synthesis of 40 years of research. *Review of Educational Research, 86,* 981–1015. https://doi.org/10.3102/0034654315626801

Index

THE PROFESSIONAL LEARNING ASSOCIATION

Learning Forward is a nonprofit, international membership association of learning educators committed to one vision in K–12 education: Equity and excellence in teaching and learning. To realize that vision, Learning Forward pursues its mission to build the capacity of leaders to establish and sustain highly effective professional learning. Information about membership, services, and products is available from www.learningforward.org.

An enduring mission

Our mission is simple but vast: Partnering to help all kids learn®. We help kids get what they need in the classroom, so they can pursue their passions, shape their future, and realize their potential.

A Sage Company

Helping educators make the greatest impact

CORWIN HAS ONE MISSION: to enhance education through intentional professional learning.

We build long-term relationships with our authors, educators, clients, and associations who partner with us to develop and continuously improve the best evidence-based practices that establish and support lifelong learning.

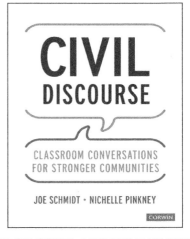

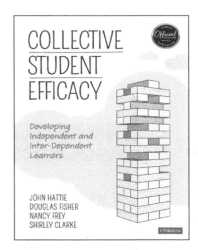

No matter where you are in your professional journey, Corwin books provide accessible strategies that benefit ALL learners—and ease the many demands teachers face.

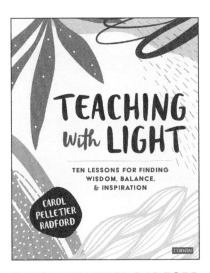

CAROL PELLETIER RADFORD

Equip teachers with the tools they need to take care of themselves so they can serve their students, step into leadership, and contribute to the education profession.

AMANDA BRUEGGEMAN

Develop student-centered approaches, promote collective efficacy, engage in coaching conversations, and prevent burnout while promoting student learning.

SERENA PARISER, VICTORIA LENTFER

Find actionable solutions to classroom management and culture, engaging lesson design, and effective communication.

STEPHANIE SMITH BUDHAI, KRISTINE S. LEWIS GRANT

Help teachers pivot instruction to ensure equitable, inclusive learning experiences in online and in-person settings.

CORWIN